The Evolving American Presidency

Series Editor

Michael A. Genovese
Loyola Chair of Leadership
Loyola Marymount University, USA

Aim of the Series

This series is stimulated by the clash between the presidency as invented and the presidency as it has developed. Over time, the presidency has evolved and grown in power, expectations, responsibilities, and authority. Adding to the power of the presidency have been wars, crises, depressions, industrialization. The importance and power of the modern presidency makes understanding it so vital. How presidents resolve challenges and paradoxes of high expectations with limited constitutional resources is the central issue in modern governance and the central theme of this book series.

More information about this series at
http://www.springer.com/series/14437

Max J. Skidmore

Presidents, Pandemics, and Politics

palgrave
macmillan

Max J. Skidmore
Political Science
University of Missouri-Kansas City
Kansas City, Kansas, USA

The Evolving American Presidency
ISBN 978-1-349-94992-2   ISBN 978-1-137-59959-9   (eBook)
DOI 10.1057/978-1-137-59959-9

Library of Congress Control Number: 2016955529

Printed on acid-free paper

This Palgrave Macmillan imprint is published by Springer Nature
The registered company is Nature America Inc. New York

Dedicated
To
Social Security Works
and to all those who struggle to protect and expand Social Security,
and to Achieve Health Care for All Americans

Contents

CONTENTS

CHAPTER 1

Introduction

Abstract This book examines major threats from disease to the people of the USA, and the ways in which American presidents have responded to such threats. It describes pandemics, and looks at several presidents. It looks critically at two, Woodrow Wilson and Dwight Eisenhower, and at their inaction when faced with influenza. It looks especially at Gerald Ford's scorned National Influenza Immunization Program (NIIP, or the Swine Flu Vaccination plan), and concludes that—in contrast to the conventional wisdom—there is much to be learned from Ford's efforts.

It discusses major achievements in combatting infectious diseases in the twentieth century, such as the eradication of smallpox, and the virtual eradication of polio and of so-called "childhood diseases," such as measles, that at one time were almost universal but are threatening to return because of the irrational refusal of many parents to immunize themselves and their children.

Above all, the book demonstrates that efforts to impose severe limits on the size, scope, and expense of government are dangerous. Government, and that means presidential action, often provides the best, and sometimes the only, method of protecting the population.

Keywords Pandemics • Presidential power • Irrationality • Vaccination • Influenza • National defense

© The Author(s) 2016
M.J. Skidmore, *Presidents, Pandemics, and Politics*, The Evolving American Presidency, DOI 10.1057/978-1-137-59959-9_1

This book examines major threats from disease to the people of the USA, and the ways in which American presidents have responded to such threats. It will look critically at two presidents who had direct roles to play in pandemics, Woodrow Wilson and Dwight Eisenhower. It will look most extensively at another who faced what appeared as though it might develop into a horrendous pandemic, but did not materialize. That president was Gerald Ford, whose National Influenza Immunization Program (NIIP) sought to vaccinate all Americans against a swine flu virus that many experts thought was impending. Without a pandemic to fight, his program was derided as a fiasco. Officials from the incoming Carter administration were triumphantly scornful of the defeated President Ford, and their scorn was exceeded by that from the forces of Ronald Reagan, who had sought to seize the nomination from the sitting president of their own party, but had failed to do so, and thus seethed with disdain for Ford's policies. This study will offer a rather favorable assessment of President Ford's program, one that is rare for reasons that it will make clear. It will consider the health policies of Presidents Clinton and Obama favorably, and will give a mixed assessment to the policies of George W. Bush: highly critical for the most part, but surprisingly favorable in others. Above all, it will make the case that guarding against pandemics is and must be an integral part of national security. Despite the book's title, now and then it will look beyond pandemics when it seems that doing so will help to evaluate presidential actions that would be relevant if the situation involved were a pandemic.

Presidents and Pandemics will argue that we must learn from past experience—mistakes and successes—in preparing for the future, and that future preparation is vital to the maintenance of civilization, here and elsewhere. As critical as terrorism is in the modern world, including bioterrorism, an even greater threat comes from natural causes. It will be necessary to overcome the tendency to respond only to the most dramatic danger—the obscenities, say, of a scowling enemy decapitating a helpless captive, attacking innocent schoolchildren, or snarling evil intent that *might* take place here—as opposed to preparation also for what assuredly *will* take place here: ever more virulent pandemics.

An examination of this kind obviously has implications not only for this country but for the rest of the world as well. The role of government will be key to national efforts; presidential understanding, commitment, and action will be prerequisite to effective government. Therefore, presidents are crucial to successful public policies.

At one time, there was little the world's population could do in the face of pandemics. Modern medicine has given us many tools to employ. The decades since the beginning of the twentieth century have been characterized, time and again, by outbreaks of new and deadly diseases that either are or have the potential to become major threats to humanity. The greatest of these to date was the misnamed "Spanish Flu" of 1918 during World War 1, a swine flu pandemic that, with a death toll of some 675,000 for this country alone, killed more Americans than even the 600,000 of the Civil War, the conflict most lethal to its citizens. Worldwide, as later chapters make clear, the pandemic's deaths exceeded those of any other cause in world history, upward of 50 million, sparing virtually no part of the planet in which there were human beings. Decades later, pandemics resulted first from Asian flu, and then from Hong Kong flu, each less lethal than its predecessor. Later in the century, despite being far less easy to transmit than influenza, came the march of HIV-AIDS. It was slower than the explosion of influenza, but its many tragic deaths were accompanied by sweeping cultural effects that were as serious as those of the wartime pandemic.

With the twenty-first century came SARS. According to the Centers for Disease Control (CDC), "Severe acute respiratory syndrome (SARS) is a viral respiratory illness caused by a coronavirus, called SARS-associated coronavirus (SARS-CoV). SARS was first reported in Asia in February 2003. The illness spread to more than two dozen countries in North America, South America, Europe, and Asia before the SARS global outbreak of 2003 was contained." Fortunately, since 2004 there have been no reported cases of SARS anywhere.[1]

In June of 2015, according to both official reports and the press, South Korea was facing the largest outbreak of MERS that had ever taken place outside of the Middle East. MERS, says the CDC, is "Middle-East Respiratory Syndrome," a severe coronavirus infection affecting human beings. The earliest reports described MERS as having been identified in 2012 in Saudi Arabia, but later corrections indicated that there had been a case a few weeks earlier in Jordan. MERS spreads from one person to another "through close contact," although the exact mechanism of transmission is not clear. It causes fever, coughing, and difficulty breathing. "About 3–4 out of every 10 patients reported with MERS have died."[2] Citing a report from The World Health Organization (WHO), the *Washington Post* said that the South Korean government was implementing "strong control measures," and that the virus—which gave no indication that it was increasing its ability to spread from one person to another—in South Korea had remained completely confined to hospitals and treatment centers.[3]

At roughly the same time there was a widespread incidence of bird flu in the USA that was causing a serious egg shortage severely affecting American restaurants. Prices escalated, and in some locations sellers began limiting egg purchases, that is, in effect they were implementing rationing of eggs.[4] *USA Today* reported that the outbreak was "especially damaging in Iowa, the nation's largest egg-producing state, with 40% of it egg-laying hens lost to the disease."[5] Government in the USA seems always to be a prime target for complaint from all segments of the political spectrum, so under the circumstances, it is hardly surprising that there was considerable criticism of the government as having done too little, too late. A spokesman from the Department of Agriculture, John Clifford, "USDA's chief veterinary officer," defended the agency before an investigating committee of the US Senate, and said that despite difficulties, the response had been quick and decisive. Also, he said, USDA had learned from the experience, and will be able to respond in ways that will "minimize the effects of this disease going forward." Iowa's two conservative Republican senators, Charles Grassley and Jodi Ernst, according to *USA Today*'s article, "have said the federal government needed to respond more quickly and offer more resources to combat the disease."[6] This is reasonable, but it seems poorly compatible with the attitudes of "small-government Republicans," especially those of Senator Ernst, who ran for office condemning dependence upon government.

This illness was not infecting human beings, but influenza affecting human beings has emerged from other animals, and seems most often to have originated among birds. Avian flu, in fact, poses perhaps the most serious potential threat that humanity faces, along with those of climate change and environmental degradation. *The New Yorker* magazine, among all the publications directed toward the most literate and highly educated segment of the reading public, seems to be most likely to deal with issues of general concern, and to do so in a thoughtful and appropriate manner. In the matter of bird flu, it did so in an article under the rubric of its occasional "Annals of Medicine."[7]

The article began with the death in Hong Kong, on 21 May 1997, of a three-year-old boy from influenza. In itself, that was not unusual, in that influenza viruses "kill hundreds of thousands of people every year. Hong Kong is among the world's most densely populated cities, and pandemics have a long history of first appearing there or in nearby regions of southern China, and then spreading rapidly around the globe."[8] What quickly became unusual, though, was the nature of the virus. An "international team of virologists," after three months of attempts, finally identified it as H5N1, an avian influenza that had killed hundreds of millions of chickens, but had not previously been known to infect a human being, even those who worked with poultry. By the end of the year, eighteen people had contracted the infection, and six had died, a "remarkably high mortality rate." Hong Kong officials worked speedily, slaughtering all the chickens in the area, and bird flu seemed to have disappeared. Officials involved included those from Hong Kong, the WHO, the CDC in Atlanta, and elsewhere. They could only have felt great relief that a worldwide pandemic had not taken place. Then, the virus appeared once more, this time in Thailand. As of 2012, it was known to have infected 587 people, killing 346 of them. This made "H5N1 one of the deadliest microbes known to medical science."[9]

The core of the piece in *The New Yorker* was a discussion of the work of a Dutch virologist, Ron Fouchier, who had succeeded in causing mutations in H5N1 that made it extremely easy to transmit, both to mammals and from mammal to mammal. Was the mere existence of this transmittable virus so dangerous to the health of the world that it should never have been created—however stringent the security imposed to keep it well contained in vaults the laboratory? Did its creation enhance potential knowledge of how to combat the virus enough to justify the creation of such a deadly organism? Critics have pointed out that dangerous organisms have escaped from the most secure facilities. Fouchier responds that nature can easily do what he did in his laboratory, and says moreover that it inevitably will do so. He concedes that bioterrorists might find ways to acquire, or create, the organism, but argues that the threat from nature itself is far greater.

Before the reports regarding the outbreak of MERS in South Korea, and bird flu in this country, there had been hysterical headlines, articles, news broadcasts, and general fear about a possible Ebola epidemic in the USA. There is no doubt regarding the deadly nature of Ebola, and there was legitimate concern about an epidemic in 2014 that raged in several West African countries, becoming the largest outbreak in history.

The serious nature of the disease, however, did not justify rampant speculation in the press and elsewhere that the virus was easily transmitted, with implications that a pandemic was inevitable. A CBS News report pointed out that much of the fear in the USA was based on misinformation and false alarms. Citing several incidents, perhaps the most extreme was that of a "schoolteacher's trip to Dallas" that was "enough to cause a panic in Maine. She was placed on medical leave after attending a conference 10 miles from the hospital where Ebola patient Thomas Eric Duncan was treated."[10] Ultimately, there were only four cases of Ebola infection in the USA, and only one of these resulted in death.[11] Because of vigorous and effective action on the part of the WHO, the governments of the African countries most affected—especially that of Liberia—and the CDC in the USA, the epidemic has been stabilized, and in Liberia actually eradicated. Nearly all the cases had occurred in only three countries, Guinea, Sierra Leone, and Liberia, and as of June 2015 those totaled fewer than 30,000. Only about 35 cases involving 15 deaths were in other countries, and on 9 May 2015 the WHO declared Liberia to be free of Ebola. That status is achieved when 42 days, or two incubation periods, have passed "since the last Ebola patient was buried."[12] Subsequently, there was another. "On June 29, routine surveillance detected a new confirmed case of Ebola in Liberia—the first confirmed case since March 20."[13]

Twentieth-Century Successes

As the twentieth century neared its end, the CDC issued a report, "Achievements in Public Health, 1900–1999 Impact of Vaccines Universally Recommended for Children—United States, 1990–1998." The report is a succinct history of improvements in public health, and contains information that should be widely recognized and appreciated.

The first vaccine to be developed was that for smallpox, and that came as early as 1796. Nevertheless, a full century later it was still not used sufficiently widely to control the disease. As the twentieth century began, vaccines against rabies, typhoid, cholera, and plague had recently been developed, but also were not yet in widespread use. As of the date of the CDC report, vaccines for twenty-one other diseases had been developed and were available, eleven of which had "been recommended for use in all U.S. children." The CDC report contains a table identifying the targeted diseases, and specifying those vaccines that had been recommended for universal childhood immunization. "National efforts to promote vaccine use among all children began with the appropriation of federal funds for polio vaccination after introduction of the vaccine in 1955. Since then federal, state, and local governments and public and private health-care providers have collaborated to develop and maintain the vaccine-delivery system in the United States."[14]

The results have been highly—even dramatically—successful. Smallpox has been eliminated, and thus the vaccine, which itself presents dangers, has been withdrawn. Polio and its associated deaths and disabilities declined dramatically, and no longer appear in the Western Hemisphere. "The last imported case caused by wild poliovirus into the United States was reported in 1993. The remaining 154 cases were vaccine-associated paralytic polio (VAPP) caused by live oral poliovirus vaccine (OPV)." It is extremely rare for OPV to cause polio, but it was unnecessary to have any risk at all. To eliminate risk entirely, OPV has not been used in the USA since 2000, only the inactivated polio virus (IPV) which cannot cause the disease.[15] Polio has thus been eliminated from the USA, and is close to being eliminated elsewhere. It is possible, though, for the disease to be re-introduced into the country by someone who has acquired it outside the country. That has happened, but not since 1993.[16]

Also declining dramatically are those that once were called "childhood diseases," such as chickenpox, mumps, and measles. Previously, these were assumed to be an almost inevitable part of growing up. Parents sometimes would have such gatherings as "chicken pox parties," or "measles parties" to expose their children to others who had the disease, and "get it over with." That obscured the danger of such infections, especially measles, which can cause permanent disabilities such as deafness, blindness, and brain damage; it can even cause death. Measles is one of the most contagious of all diseases. With regard to measles vaccine and the extent of transmittability, the CDC says, "Measles spreads when a person infected with the measles virus breathes, coughs, or sneezes. It is very contagious. You can catch measles just by being in a room where a person with measles has been, up to 2 hours after that person is gone. And you can catch measles from an infected person even before they have a measles rash. Almost everyone who has not had the MMR shot will get measles if they are exposed to the measles virus."[17] "MMR" refers to the combined vaccination for measles, mumps, and rubella. It is responsible for one of the largest improvements in public health overall. In 2000, the USA had achieved "measles elimination," although a few cases continued to occur from importation of the virus by travelers.[18]

A Disturbing Development

Although there is no question regarding the enormous improvement in public health that has resulted from the widespread use of vaccines, an anti-vaccination movement has developed reflecting two different themes. One is religious belief, often supported by anti-government attitudes that oppose government intrusion into personal practice and belief. The other has coalesced within better-educated groups who nevertheless base their conclusions on poor science, and emotionally-charged arguments. The Internet has been a major factor in spreading misinformation.

If a child is autistic and has been vaccinated, there is a tendency for its parent to be receptive when someone argues that "vaccinations cause autism," a connection for which there is no scientific evidence whatever. In response to the scientific argument that no evidence exists to suggest a link, it is easy to twist logic to say that no proof exists that vaccines do *not* cause autism, ignoring all questions regarding proof of negatives. Other allegations for which there is no scientific evidence are that vaccines cause autism and other ailments by "overloading" a child's immune system, or that somehow "natural" immunity is better than the immunity that bodies develop in response to vaccines.

There can be a community of interest here between right-wing groups who oppose government social programs in principle and left-leaning groups who favor the idea of such programs, but who fear the influence of large corporations and other financial interests, their influence on government, and their control of established institutions. One does not have to be a leftist to decry the influence of the powerful. It was, after all, no radical but an essentially conservative American president and five-star general, Dwight D. Eisenhower, who warned in his farewell speech about the "military-industrial complex." Such an awareness of the influence of anti-democratic forces is rational. It is even essential to maintain democracy, but it does not justify complete cynicism. It is highly irrational to conclude that the obvious influence of money on politics must mean that all information from any official source or institution is invalid, or that any action must be self-serving.

Such a view becomes what the late historian Richard Hofstadter called "the paranoid style" in American politics.[19] His point was that of course there are conspiracies in history, but it nevertheless is irrational to the point of delusion to believe that the whole of history is a conspiracy. The characteristics of much of the literature generated by the anti-vaccination groups and the writings that influence them are uncomfortably close to those generated by groups that most intelligent observers would have to classify as cults.

There are many thoughtful analyses of the controversy, but one of the most cogent is by Peter Salk, in *The Atlantic*, "The Anti-Vaccine Movement is Forgetting the Polio Epidemic."[20] Peter Salk is a distinguished medical researcher himself who is the son of the originator of the polio vaccine, Jonas Salk. One should remember that Jonas Salk could have patented the Salk vaccine, and made literally billions of dollars from it. He did not even consider doing so, though, because he believed the vaccine should belong to the people.

With regard to measles, the USA in 2015 had its first fatality from the disease since 2003. In late 2014, an outbreak of the disease took place in California as a result of exposure at a theme park. It was responsible for 117 cases in several states; the total measles cases in the first six months of 2015 came from five outbreaks and appeared in 24 states, and amounted to 178 (including the 117).[21] As a result of the diminishing number of people being vaccinated and the increasing number of measles cases, California, on 30 June 2015, passed a strict new vaccination law requiring vaccinations for schoolchildren and eliminating exemptions because of personal belief or religious reasons; only medical reasons can now justify an exemption. Upon signing the bill into law, Governor Jerry Brown remarked, "The science is clear that vaccines dramatically protect children against a number of infectious and dangerous diseases," ... "While it is true that no medical intervention is without risk, the evidence shows that immunization powerfully benefits and protects the community." California thus joined only two other states, Mississippi and West Virginia, in requiring all schoolchildren regardless of religion or personal belief to be vaccinated unless there are legitimate medical reasons that justify exempting a child.[22] Outraged by the new law, parents and others who oppose vaccination indicated that they would immediately begin a campaign to repeal the new statute.

THE IMPORTANCE OF NATIONAL, AND PRESIDENTIAL, ACTION

We are dealing here with no less than the essential elements of national (and worldwide) defense. Most of these principles are self-evident, and many are being employed here and elsewhere. The connection between health and national defense should be self-evident. An interesting article by Chuck

Brooks of the Xerox Corporation makes clear the roles already played by the "many organizations that play significant roles in warning, treating, and protecting against infectious outbreaks. The World Health Organization, Centers for Disease Control and Prevention, the Health and Human Services and Defense Departments are all experienced with the challenges that may arise when dealing with worldwide pandemic events."[23] Brooks, in his capacity at Xerox as Vice President/Client Executive, works directly with the Department of Homeland Security (DHS), demonstrating the close ties between public and private organizations with regard to protecting the population.

The mission of the Department of Homeland Security concentrates upon defense against terrorism, but its activities are relevant to natural threats as well. Brooks describes the segments within DHS of the Office of Health Affairs, and the Chemical and Biological Defense Division of Science and Technology Directorate, which "provide comprehensive analysis of threat characterization," and the like. Examples of relevant programs include "Foreign Animal Defense Vaccines and Diagnostics," which works in cooperation with the Department of Agriculture and the National Bio-and Agro-Defense Facility in Manhattan, Kansas; Underground Transportation Restoration, aimed at maintaining transportation capabilities after biological events; and risk assessments. Broadening beyond military considerations, he recognizes natural threats as relevant, and mentions infectious Ebola as demonstrating "the threat of *pandemics* and bioterrorism" (italics added). Earlier recent threats of possible epidemics came in 2002 and 2003 from SARS, possible terrorist attacks came in 2001 from Anthrax scares, "and the 2004 ricin letters. Many forget," he wrote, "that the 1918 Spanish Flu influenza pandemic killed more than 50,000 [*sic*; this likely was a misprint from 50,000,000] people. We are all vulnerable and the vigilance to bio threats are [sic] necessary and should not be taken lightly." His final sentence sums it up: "Pandemics, whether they are generated by nature or terrorists need to be addressed through interagency preparedness, training, and communication..."[24] The additional point around which this book revolves is that we must learn from past experiences, and view them objectively rather than from partisan or ideologically tainted perspectives.

The greatest rejection of the need for a strong government role is likely to come from within the USA, where there is resistance to scientific findings on such things as vaccination and climate change, and where scientific issues such as these have been made into political issues.

In summary, given the nature of biological threats, *governments must take the lead in developing and implementing strategies to protect the world's populations.* Official international organizations also must employ their resources fully. Regarding national defense, protection against pandemic illness is at least as urgent a matter as is military preparedness. This is true regardless of the source of the threat, but the greatest threats are from nature itself.

Of all the world's countries, the USA is the most powerful, and has the greatest resources. Therefore, *America's government must take a lead in marshaling protective forces, developing and implementing strategies, and creating and encouraging the creation of the knowledge required to deal with potential catastrophes.*

The unique nature of America's government is such that it *requires a strong, active, and dedicated president and executive branch, if it is to be effective.* It is not by accident that one author titled his work on the presidency "The Ferocious Engine of Democracy: A History of the American Presidency."[25]

Because of this, the traditional American disdain for government must give way to a recognition that, *although controls on government are essential, a strong and active government is also essential.* The acceptance by one of America's two major parties of former President Reagan's firm belief that "government is not the solution," and that government, itself, is the problem, is potentially a greater threat to the people of America and elsewhere than are the actions of terrorists. The assumption that keeping taxes low is more important than any government responsibility and function must be recognized as irrational.

NOTES

1. Centers for Disease Control and Prevention, "Severe Acute Respiratory Syndrome (SARS)," http://www.cdc.gov/sars/; retrieved 11 July 2015.
2. Centers for Disease Control and Prevention, "Middle East Respiratory Syndrome (MERS)," Page last updated June 5, 2015; http://www.cdc.gov/coronavirus/mers/about/; retrieved 3 July 2015.
3. Kim Tong-Hyung, "WHO: MERS Not Spreading Outside S. Korea Hospitals," *Washington Post* (13 June 1015); http://www.washington-post.com/world/middle_east/who-mers-not-spreading-outside-s-korea-hospitals/2015/06/13/9995f426-1230-11e5-a0fe-dccfea4653ee_story.html; retrieved 3 July 2015.

4. Roberto Ferdman, "Egg Rationing in America has Officially Begun," *Washington Post* (5 June 2015); http://www.washingtonpost.com/blogs/wonkblog/wp/2015/06/05/the-largest-grocer-in-the-texas-is-now-rationing-eggs/; retrieved 4 July 2015.

5. Christopher Doering, "Egg, Poultry Groups Criticize USDA's Handling of Bird Flu Outbreak," *USA Today* (8 July 2015); http://www.usatoday.com/story/news/nation/2015/07/07/senate-committee-considers-impact-of-bird-flu/29823229/; retrieved 10 July 2015.

6. *Ibid.*

7. See, Michael Specter, "The Deadliest Virus," *The New Yorker* (12 March 2012).

8. *Ibid.*

9. *Ibid.*

10. Carter Evans, "Ebola Panic Spreading Much Faster than Disease in U.S.," *CBS News* (18 October 2014); http://www.cbsnews.com/news/ebola-panic-in-us-spreading-much-faster-than-disease/; retrieved 4 July 2015.

11. Centers for Disease Control and Prevention, "2014 Ebola Outbreak in West Africa – Case Counts," (updated July 2, 2015); http://www.cdc.gov/vhf/ebola/outbreaks/2014-west-africa/case-counts.html; retrieved 4 July 2015.

12. *Ibid.*

13. Centers for Disease Control and Prevention, "2014 Ebola Outbreak in West Africa – Outbreak Update," (1 July 2015); http://www.cdc.gov/vhf/ebola/outbreaks/2014-west-africa/index.html; retrieved 4 July 2015.

14. Centers for Disease Control and Prevention, "Achievements in Public Health, 1900-1999 Impact of Vaccines Universally Recommended for Children—United States, 1990–1998" (2 April 1999); http://www.cdc.gov/mmwr/preview/mmwrhtml/00056803.htm; retrieved 14 July 2015; vaccines identified in Table One.

15. Centers for Disease Control and Prevention, "Polio Disease – Questions and Answers," (11 August 2014) http://www.cdc.gov/vaccines/vpd-vac/polio/dis-faqs.htm; retrieved 14 July 2015.

16. Centers for Disease Control and Prevention, "Polio Elimination in the United States" (29 May 2015) http://www.cdc.gov/polio/us/index.html; retrieved 14 July 2015.

17. Centers for Disease Control and Prevention, "Vaccines and Immunization" (7 April 2015) http://www.cdc.gov/vaccines/vpd-vac/measles/fs-parents.html; retrieved 14 July 2015.

18. Centers for Disease Control and Prevention, "CDC Advisory," *HAN (Health Alert Network)* 23 January 2015 http://emergency.cdc.gov/han/han00376.asp; retrieved 15 July 2015.

19. Richard Hofstader, *The Paranoid Style in American Politics*, Cambridge: Harvard University Press 1964; available in numerous subsequent editions.
20. Peter Salk, "The Anti-Vaccine Movement is Forgetting the Polio Epidemic," *The Atlantic* (28 October 2014).
21. Centers for Disease Control and Prevention, "Measles Cases and Outbreaks," (30 June 2015) http://www.cdc.gov/measles/cases-outbreaks.html; retrieved 15 July 2015.
22. Adam Nagourney, "California Mandates Vaccines for Schoolchildren," *The New York Times* (30 June 2015). P. A 19.
23. Chuck Brooks, "The DHS's Role in Confronting Pandemics an Bioterrorism," *Federal Times* (22 December 2014; originally published 4 November) http://www.federaltimes.com/story/government/dhs/blog/2014/12/22/dhs-role-in-confronting-pandemics-and-bioterroreism/20770335/; retrieved 15 July 2015.
24. *Ibid.*
25. Michael Riccards, *The Ferocious Engine of Democracy: A History of the American Presidency*, 2 volumes, New York: Madison Books, 1995.

CHAPTER 2

Pandemic Influenza

Abstract This chapter deals with the nature of pandemic influenza, and demonstrates that in spite of the cavalier approach that frequently characterizes popular attitudes ("Oh, it's nothing, just a touch of the flu"), influenza is a serious disease that must not be taken lightly. In fact, influenza caused the greatest pandemic in humanity's history in terms of the actual number of deaths. The misnamed "Spanish Flu" of 1918, in contrast to most influenza pandemics that target infants and the elderly, hit especially hard among younger adults, and caused more deaths than any great war. Worldwide, it killed more than the Second World War, and did so in a brief period.

What happened before can happen again, and given the nature of influenza, it could recur in even more virulent form. Moreover, there are other viral infections that could ultimately prove to be even more of a threat.

America expends considerable resources guarding against terrorist attacks that might occur. This is appropriate, but what is not appropriate is that the country spends relatively little against pandemics that assuredly will take place at some time.

Keywords Ebola • "Spanish flu" • Popular culture • Literature • History • Death toll from flu

© The Author(s) 2016
M.J. Skidmore, *Presidents, Pandemics, and Politics*, The Evolving American Presidency, DOI 10.1057/978-1-137-59959-9_2

Influenza Is Not to Be Taken Lightly

A clear understanding of the situation must first rest upon recognition that, as health professionals are well aware, influenza, even under normal circumstances, is not a benign disease. Recent attention to the possibility of an outbreak of avian flu—or "bird flu"—may to some extent have increased public awareness of its disastrous potential, but it is still common to hear influenza dismissed as little more than a mere inconvenience, as in "Oh, it's nothing much; just a touch of the flu."

Cavalier attitudes notwithstanding, "CDC scientists estimate that an average of 36,000 people...die from influenza-related complications each year in the United States."[1] That is, in each *normal* year, and in each of those normal years, influenza results in some 200,000 hospital admissions. These figures are hardly trivial. To be sure, they are imprecise. Many of the deaths result from pneumonia and other respiratory complications that accompany influenza, thus creating ground for questioning whether so many deaths "really" result from the flu.[2] On the other hand, one does not have to search hard to discover assertions in print that in a normal year the death toll may be greater yet.

As is often the case, precision is elusive, but for our purposes, it is also unnecessary. The clear and important fact is that influenza is a serious illness that causes numerous deaths even in an ordinary year—and some years are far from ordinary. The Asian flu pandemic, for example, was responsible in 1957 for some 80,000 deaths in the USA, and around two million worldwide.[3] Even though he noted the American death toll, and wrote that the Asian flu "sickened some 25 to 30 percent of the American population," Adam Volland in *U.S. News and World Report* could say that the 1957 strain "wasn't particularly potent."[4] Perhaps not, and certainly not in comparison with what had taken place nearly four decades before, but those who suffered and survived the 1957 pandemic can attest to the truly debilitating nature of the Asian flu while it lasted.

A personal note may be in order here. I was in graduate school, at that time, and remember being incredibly ill, probably the sickest I have ever been, and for several days. My wife was unable to eat or drink anything, even a sip of water, without vomiting. Her nausea had lasted three days. The doctor who examined her at her bedside—those were the days when physicians still made house calls—said that the next morning he would have to order her hospitalized, unless she began to be able to take fluids and nourishment. Fortunately, by then she had begun to tolerate sips of water and a few bites of a bland cookie normally sold for babies. "Debilitating" hardly describes the violent nature of the illness, as strong as that word is. It is not something that one forgets.

INFLUENZA AT ITS MOST HORRENDOUS—SO FAR

The Asian flu pandemic was neither the worst nor the mildest of the influenza pandemics of the century. John M. Barry, historian and journalist, has produced the definitive study of the worst, the "Spanish Flu" that erupted in 1918, and swept the world quickly in three waves. Barry's work reflects deep immersion in the subject, so great that it inspired praise from the American Medical Association, and brought him relevant academic appointments (such as the post of visiting scholar at the Center for Bioenvironmental Research at Tulane and Xavier Universities).

"Not all pandemics are lethal," he pointed out, and described the three that swept around the world in the century that recently ended. "The most recent new virus attacked in 1968, when the H3N2 'Hong Kong flu' spread worldwide, with high morbidity but very low mortality—that is, it made many sick, but killed few," he said. "The 'Asian flu,' an H2N2 virus, came in 1957; while nothing like 1918, this was still a violent pandemic. Then of course there was the H1N1 virus of 1918, the virus that created its own killing fields."[5] It was this fierce pandemic—the so-called (and misnamed) "Spanish Flu"—that led the Ford administration to launch its NIIP when a new swine flu virus was discovered that appeared to be similar to the agent that caused the 1918 pandemic.

Never had anything in humanity's entire history—war, famine, pestilence, or anything else—infected so many human beings, and killed so many in such a brief period. "In 1927, a scholar put the Spanish Flu's global mortality at 21.5 million. In 1991, a systematic recalculation raised it to 30 million. A later estimate, published in the *Bulletin of the History of Medicine*, sets the minimum mortality at 50 million, with an upper limit of 100 million."[6] Deaths from the Spanish Flu, a worldwide pandemic in roughly one year, were at least equal in number to the entire death toll a generation later from the greatest war humanity has ever fought, the Second World War; most likely, in fact, flu deaths in 1918 had been far greater in number than those from the later war. Note, also, that World War II took more than six times as long as the Spanish Flu to produce its total deaths. During the 1918 pandemic, an estimated one-third of the entire population of the world at the time, somewhere around 500 million people, "were infected and had clinically apparent illnesses."[7] To be sure, the plague in the 1300s killed a far greater portion of the population (at least the European population). More than one of every four Europeans died, "but in raw numbers influenza killed more than plague then, more than AIDS today."[8]

The name "Spanish Flu" came to be applied to the disease because its toll in Spain was great. This was "to Spain's consternation. After all, other countries of Europe, as well as the United States and countries in Asia, were hit too in that spring of 1918. Maybe the name stuck because Spain, still unaligned, did not censor its news reports, unlike other European countries. And so Spain's flu was no secret, unlike the flu elsewhere."[9]

The point of origin almost certainly was not Spain, and in fact seems to have been in the USA. Barry traces it back to Kansas, and believes it originated early in 1918 in Haskell County. He says that the evidence suggests that from there the "virus traveled east across the state to a huge army base, and from there to Europe, through South America, through Asia and Africa, through isolated islands in the Pacific, through all the wide world."[10]

By whatever name, the influenza of 1918 was devastating. When victims of most strains of influenza die, the likely cause is pneumonia or some other secondary infection that the flu-weakened patient is too weak to withstand. The 1918 flu killed directly. Of course, it was also responsible for deaths from secondary causes. Most strains of influenza, as one would expect, cause the greatest number of casualties among the elderly and the very young. For reasons that even now are not clear, the 1918 flu tended to strike young, healthy, adults. "The attack rate and mortality was highest among adults 20 to 50 years old."[11] And it hit quickly. Many times a strong, young, man or woman would awaken feeling healthy and well, only to become "sick by noon," and die "by nightfall."[12] Infants and the elderly did die, but "in 1918 the great spike came in the middle. In 1918 an age graph of the dead would look like a W."[13]

The pain was unbearable. "Patients would writhe from agonizing pain in their joints." They would "suffer extreme fever and chills, shuddering, shivering, then huddling under blankets." Intense pains throughout the body mimicked those from other diseases. There was often spontaneous bleeding from every orifice. Extraordinary earaches and pain seeming to come from pressure within the head were common, as was debilitating pain behind the eyes accompanied by visual disturbances. "Pockets of air leaking through ruptured lungs made patients crackle when they were rolled onto their sides. One navy nurse later compared the sound to a bowl of rice crispies [sic], and the memory of that sound was so vivid to her that for the rest of her life she could not tolerate being around anyone who was eating rice crispies [sic]."[14] Oxygen deprivation, or cyanosis, was so complete that the bodies of those who died had often turned a dark blue, so dark that it was sometimes impossible to tell whether the victim had been white or black. Many of those who survived suffered lifelong damage. The total number of American deaths resulting from the Spanish Flu has been reported to have been as high as 675,000.[15] "Nearly half of all deaths in the United States in 1918 were flu related."[16]

In view of the enormous dimensions of the tragedy, it is astonishing that it seemed quickly to have faded from popular memory. Health professionals are under no illusion regarding the danger from influenza, but even with publicity that has been given in the last decade to the possibility of an avian flu pandemic, there seems still to be a popular tendency to disregard influenza as a major threat to life. A US Navy nurse, Carla Morrisey, in 1986 wrote of the 1918 pandemic in *Navy Medicine*.[17] She based her article on "an oral history provided by Josie Mabel Brown, a Navy nurse who served at Great Lakes Naval Hospital during the height of the epidemic." Morrisey was commemorating her great aunt's—Ms Brown's—100th birthday. She noted that the 1918 flu "now seems merely a folk memory," and pondered why it was that "Americans took little notice of the epidemic and then quickly forgot what they did notice." She said that "the formal histories, magazines, newspapers, and military journals notably ignored the epidemic. Little was noticed and recorded for later generations." On the other hand, in personal papers, reminiscences, "autobiographies of people who were not in authority," and the like, "it is apparent that the individual was frightened and his life dramatically changed."[18] She quoted a rhyme that young girls all over the country would chant as they skipped rope:

I had a bird and his name was Enza.
I opened the window and
In-flu-enza.[19]

Part of the reason for the relative lack of attention, she speculated, was that mass deaths from disease in those days prior to modern medicine were almost a way of life. Also, along with others, she pointed out that the horrors of the pandemic and those of the First World War were almost wrapped together as a single phenomenon.[20]

Nevertheless, the pandemic's effect on the people was so huge as to be difficult to exaggerate, and it did spur enormous activity "among medical scientists and their institutions." But this was "the single great exception. It did not lead to great changes in government, armies, and corporations. It had little influence on the course of political and military events."[21] In searching for an explanation, she quoted a comment from H. L. Mencken as the possible reason. "The human mind," he said, "always tries to expunge the intolerable from memory, just as it tries to conceal it while current."

Other authorities also speculate on the virtual vanishing of the pandemic from the collective memory. The thoughtful and insightful historian and geographer Alfred W. Crosby pointed out that because of the flu's death toll, the average American life expectancy in the year 1918 tumbled by 20 years.[22] He thought it remarkable that despite the vast toll in health and even life, the pandemic seemed suddenly to disappear from consciousness. As he pointed out in an extended musing that he called "An Inquiry into the Peculiarities of Human Memory," there was little mention of the tragedy in either history or literature.[23] He believed the war to have been the major cause. He, too, said that many thought of the pandemic as simply a subdivision of the war.[24]

Only occasionally does a writer of that rich literary period allude even briefly to the flu, and it took the traumatic death of his brother, Benjamin Harrison Wolfe, to induce Thomas Wolfe to craft a chapter in his novel *Look Homeward Angel* using the illness as its theme.[25] There was, however, one major exception in literature, Katherine Anne Porter's *Pale Horse, Pale Rider*. Crosby accurately describes it as a "masterpiece of short fiction."[26]

Porter's work is a brief trilogy of novellas, the third of which is "Pale Horse, Pale Rider," from which the whole takes its name. Crosby writes, correctly, that it is "the most accurate depiction of American society in the fall of 1918 in literature. It synthesizes what is otherwise only obtainable by reading hundreds of pages of newspapers." Regardless of that, historians have paid it no attention at all.[27]

Porter based her portrait of the time on her own experience as a victim of the flu who nearly died. She was so ill that "her obituary was set in type. She recovered. Her fiancé did not." Barry describes her "haunting novella" as one of the best—and one of the few—sources for what life was like during the disease."[28]

It is even more than that. Porter also presented a glimpse of what life was like in Wilson's wartime America, which at least on a national scale probably came closer to totalitarianism than the country has ever been, before or since. (On a regional basis the ante-bellum South had also closed ranks to impose a relentless conformity in its efforts to defend slavery, and it continued its solidarity for a century afterward.) In the Wilson era, this authoritarianism in no way reflected a proto-fascist ideology, but rather a malady that can easily affect democracies: a determined effort to direct all attention to a war effort. The Espionage and Sedition Acts are reasonably well-known, as are some of the period's other governmental excesses such as the Palmer Raids, but the authoritarian dynamics were not exclusive to government; they existed also at the personal level, and sometimes mixed the personal with the official as in the case of the American Protective League, "a secret service volunteer division of the Department of Justice."[29] Porter's main character in *Pale Horse, Pale Rider*, Miranda, was a young and underpaid journalist making only $18 a week. She was berated, and feared for her job or worse, because she could not afford to pay $50 to buy a Liberty Bond.[30]

The novelist Alice McDermott praised Porter's fine work in a brief segment on NPR's "All Things Considered." She had assigned the book to her graduate students at Johns Hopkins University, she said, and one student obtained a lovely, hardbound edition of the 1939 work online. It turned out to be a library discard, stamped "Out of Date, Low Demand." McDermott titled her presentation, "Why Libraries Should Stock *Pale Horse, Pale Rider*."[31]

Porter figured prominently in the 1998 PBS documentary "Influenza 1918," for the series *This American Life*, in 1998,[32] but the emphasis was on her life, not its fictional portrayal in *Pale Horse, Pale Rider*. The documentary mentioned the obituary for which her newspaper "quietly set the type." It even said that "her fever rose so high that her hair turned white, then fell out." Crosby mentioned that as well.[33] The dramatic production was powerful (if incomplete), using photographs and visual images along with skillful narrative. It quoted Dr. Victor Vaughn, Surgeon General of the Army, who feared that the disease could cause civilization "to disappear from the face of the earth within a few weeks." But something happened: "just as suddenly as it struck, the calamitous disease abruptly began to vanish." Why? A Los Angeles County public health official, Dr. Shirley Fannin, provided a likely explanation based on modern understanding of influenza. She said that the disease "probably ran out of fuel. It ran out of people who were susceptible and could be infected." Although it noted that the tragedy changed the lives of survivors, such as Porter, forever, this documentary, too, marveled that "World War I and painful memories associated with the epidemic caused it to be mostly forgotten."

To a great extent, and in spite of recent books, documentaries, and warnings about avian flu, the general public still appears to have little knowledge of the horrors in our relatively recent past. Barry agrees with others regarding the reason, saying that "the relative lack of impact it left on literature may not be unusual at all. It may not be that much unlike what happened centuries ago." One scholar of medieval literature, Barry wrote, said that "while there are a few vivid and terrifying accounts, it's actually striking how little was written on the bubonic plague. Outside of these few very well-known accounts, there is almost nothing in literature about it afterwards." Barry speculates that writers deal well with the horrors that people inflict on people, but that they apparently "forget the horrors that nature inflicts on people, the horrors that make humans less significant."[34]

Perhaps he is correct. Despite the recent, and short-lived, near hysteria about Ebola, can there be any doubt that after years of propaganda following 9/11, Americans have been far more worried about possible actions from terrorists than about any threat from a pandemic? This is true even though terrorists at their worst likely present a danger that pales into insignificance beside the 1918 flu, or beyond the real possibility of an even more virulent disease.

NOTES

1. CDC (Centers for Disease Control and Prevention), 2003, "CDC Finds Annual Flu Deaths Higher Than Previously Estimated," Press Release (7 January 2003).
2. See, e.g., Anita Manning, "Study: Annual Flu Death Toll Could be Overstated." USA Today, (11 December 2005); http://usatoday30.usa-today.com/news/health/2005-12-11-flu-deaths_x.htm; retrieved 7 June 2015.
3. Mike Davis, The Monster at Our Door: The Global Threat of Avian Flu. New York: Henry Holt, 2006. p. 36.
4. Adam Volland, "Lessons From a Bug: A Pandemic Filled Beds but Offered Important Insights," U.S. News and World Report (20 August 2007), p. 69.

5. John M. Barry, *The Great Influenza*. New York: Penguin Books, 2005, p. 115.
6. See David Brown, 2002, "A Shot in the Dark: Swine Flu's Vaccine Lessons." *Washington Post* (27 May 2002), p. A 9; see also Niall Johnson, and Müller Jürgen, 2002, "Updating the Accounts: Global Mortality of the 1918–1920 'Spanish' Influenza Pandemic," *Bulletin of the History of Medicine*, 76:1, (2002), pp. 105–115.
7. Jeffry K. Taubenberger, and David M. Morens, "History: 1918 Influenza: The Mother of all Pandemics," *Emerging Infectious Diseases (CDC)*, 12:1 (January 2006); p. 1; http://www.ncbi.nlm.nih.gov/pmc/articles/PMC3291398/; retrieved 7 June 2015.
8. Barry, p. 4.
9. Gina Kolata, *Flu: The Story of the Great Influenza Pandemic of 1918 and the Search for the Virus that Caused it*, New York: Touchstone (Simon and Schuster), 2005, p. 10.
10. Barry, p. 92.
11. "Pandemics and Pandemic Scares in the 20th Century," National Vaccine Program Office, Department of Health and Human Services (12 February 2004); p. 1; http://archive.hhs.gov/nvpo/pandemics/flu3.htm ; retrieved 7 June 2015.
12. *Ibid.*
13. Barry, p. 239.
14. *Ibid.*, pp. 234–235.
15. Jeffry K. Taubenberger, "Chasing the Elusive 1918 Virus: Preparing for the Future by Examining the Past." *The Threat of Pandemic Influenza: Workshop Summary*. Washington: National Academies Press (Institute of Medicine), (2005), pp. 69–89; reference, p. 73.
16. Laurie Garrett, "The Next Pandemic?" *Foreign Affairs* (July/August 2005), p. 2; also available at http://www.foreignaffairs.org.
17. Carla R. Morrisey, "The Influenza Epidemic of 1918." *Navy Medicine* 77:3 (May–June 1986), pp. 11–17; http://www.history.navy.mil/research/library/online-reading-room/title-list-alphabetically/i/influenza/the-influenza-epidemic-of-1918-by-carla-r-morrisey-rn-bsn.html; retrieved 7 June 2015.
18. *Ibid.*, pp. 11–13.
19. *Ibid.*, p. 14.
20. *Ibid.*, p. 12.
21. *Ibid.*, p. 14.
22. Alfred W. Crosby, *America's Forgotten Pandemic: The Influenza of 1918*, Cambridge, England: Cambridge University Press, 2003. P. xi.
23. *Ibid.*, pp. 311–328.
24. *Ibid.*, p. 320.

25. Thomas Wolfe, *Look Homeward Angel,* New York: Simon and Schuster, 1929; mentioned *Ibid.,* pp. 315–317.
26. Crosby, p. 318.
27. *Ibid.*
28. Barry, p. 394.
29. See Max J. Skidmore, *Moose Crossing: Portland to Portland on the Theodore Roosevelt International Highway,* Lanham, Maryland: Hamilton Books, 2007, p. 106.
30. Katherine Anne Porter, *Pale Horse, Pale Rider,* New York: Harcourt Brace, 1939, pp. 144–148.
31. McDermott, Alice, 2006. "Why Libraries Should Stock *Pale Horse, Pale Rider.*" NPR, *All Things Considered,* 23 October 2006.
32. "Influenza 1918," *This American Life,* PBS, 1998; program description, complete transcript, etc., at http://www.pbs.org/wgbh/americanexperience/films/influenza/; retrieved 7 June 2015; available on DVD from PBS.
33. Crosby, pp. 317–318.
34. Barry, p. 394.

CHAPTER 3

Misguided Responses to Public Health Emergencies

Abstract This chapter considers some misguided responses to public health emergencies, or perceived emergencies. At one extreme was the arrest and lifetime confinement in Hawaii and elsewhere of sufferers from leprosy, or Hansen's disease. This, of course, was not an example of presidential policy, but is included as an example of horrible overreach.

An opposite approach was the refusal of the Eisenhower administration to mount a vaccination program to deal with the Asian flu pandemic of 1957. President Eisenhower was devoted to private solutions to such emergencies, and these were manifestly inadequate.

There was yet another extreme example of a misguided approach, and that was President Woodrow Wilson's militant passivity to the 1918 influenza pandemic. Disregarding advice from medical consultants, he refused to discontinue the shipment of troops abroad to fight in the Great War, which resulted in an even greater spread of the contagion because of the great numbers of men confined to small quarters aboard ships.

Incompetence can always be a danger in public health emergencies. Although this was not a pandemic, the George W. Bush administration handled the health crisis caused by Hurricane Katrina so poorly that it became a national scandal. On the other hand, President Bush did move to plan wisely for a possible influenza pandemic when he ordered the creation of national stockpiles of antiviral medication.

© The Author(s) 2016   25
M.J. Skidmore, *Presidents, Pandemics, and Politics,* The Evolving
American Presidency, DOI 10.1057/978-1-137-59959-9_3

Keywords Over reaction • Under reaction • Great War • Pandemics • Spanish flu • Asian flu • Theodore Roosevelt • Woodrow Wilson • Dwight Eisenhower • G.W. Bush administration • Katrina

Public health emergencies, or perceived emergencies, throughout history have brought a variety of official responses. Some of these have been effective, some have not. Some have been rational, some have not. Societies have often been tempted by, and given in to, one of two dangerous extremes: over-reaction on the one hand, or inaction on the other. American history is replete with examples; it is useful to examine a few of the more relevant.

Understandably, one method that societies have often adopted is quarantine. In its long history quarantine has sometimes been effective; sometimes not. It has sometimes been warranted, sometimes not. In 2004, PBS broadcast a program on quarantine that provided a quick look throughout history.[1] In any case, regardless of whether it has been appropriate or effective, quarantine by its very nature has strong political implications.

The Tragedies of Kalaupapa and Carville

Although it was far from typical, an extreme version of quarantine constituted one of the greatest over-reactions in American history. At the least, this sad episode should serve as a warning against the kind of excess that many people advocate when faced with newly threatening circumstances, such as HIV-AIDS, SARS, or Ebola. This particular over-reaction was the treatment of those who suffered from Hansen's disease, or leprosy. The disease "results in damage primarily to the peripheral nerves (the nerves outside the brain and spinal cord), skin, testes, eyes, and mucous membrane of the nose. Because of the visible disfigurement…people with leprosy have long been feared and shunned."[2]

The harsh treatment imposed upon those afflicted with leprosy began in 1865, when Hawaii's King Kamehameha V signed "An Act to Prevent the Spread of Leprosy." Under the act's provisions, the Board of Health was directed not only to arrest the victims of Hansen's disease but also to remove them from the general population—permanently. The colony, Kalaupapa, ultimately became the permanent prison for victims of leprosy. It was situated on the island of Moloka'i. At that time, of course, Hawaii was an independent Pacific kingdom, and not yet American. When the USA annexed Hawaii at the end of the century, the draconian quarantine restrictions remained in place, thus becoming perhaps the most notorious over-reaction to a disease in America's history. They remained for a time, even after Hawaii became a state.

Moloka'i is an elongated island about ten miles wide, stretching some 38 miles east and west. In the middle, the Makanalua Peninsula forms the northern shore. The peninsula is flat, and separated from the main body of Moloka'i by cliffs reaching nearly 2000 feet in height. The peninsula's eastern section is the district of Kalawao. Kalaupapa is in the west. It is here that the Hawaiian government located its colony for those afflicted with Hansen's disease. There are no roads connecting the peninsula with the rest of the island, only a rugged mountain path. The cliffs form a substantial barrier, completing the isolation of the area surrounded on three sides by ocean. There are two places suitable for landing by water, in Kalaupapa and Kalawao, and there is now a small airstrip. Thus, practically speaking, access must be by air or sea.

Even by Hawaiian standards, the beauty is stunning. In March of 2007 I had the good fortune to visit Molokai and Kalaupapa. The following discussion is based upon, or enhanced by, my observations and conversations there at that time. The stark injustice and deep sorrow of those condemned to spend their lives in isolation—through no fault of their own—is equally stunning. So that their history will never be forgotten, the area has been given to the National Park Service. The human costs of removing its sufferers were extraordinary; as greater knowledge of the disease developed, it also became clear that they were unnecessary. Modern medical science has demonstrated that Hansen's disease "is not highly contagious, does not cause death, and can be effectively treated with antibiotics."[3]

Many people had thought all along that the contagion had been exaggerated. A century ago, the writer Jack London wrote a series of articles for *Woman's Home Companion* magazine, discussing his five-day stay in the Kalaupapa colony. "The Lepers of Molokai," the first of these, appeared in January, 1908.[4] One should note that those infected with the disease consider the term "leper" to be highly offensive.[5]

"Leprosy is not so contagious as is imagined," London wrote, and added, "I went for a week's visit to the Settlement, and I took my wife along—all of which would have not happened had we had any apprehension of contracting the disease. Nor did we wear long, gauntleted gloves and keep apart from the lepers. On the contrary, we mingled freely with them."[6] London decried the treatment that victims of the disease had received throughout history, and said that the "awful horror" with which they have been regarded "in the past" and the "frightful treatment" that they had received were "unnecessary and cruel."

Astonishingly, though, he was still capable of writing this incredible sentence: "That a leper is unclean, however, should be insisted upon; and the segregation of lepers, from what little is known of the disease, should be rigidly maintained." It should therefore come as no surprise that he disputed accounts of shock and grief involved, and that he minimized any trauma that the victims experienced when taken from their society and relocated to Kalaupapa. Under the circumstances, it might have been expected that he would present a highly romanticized view of life in the Kalaupapa community, and he certainly did so. His articles bring to mind some of the more discreet examples of antebellum Southern apologies for slavery, and they also foreshadowed some of the arguments justifying racial segregation that came from opponents during the Civil Rights Movement.

Scientists identified the cause of Hansen's disease, the bacterium "mycobacterium leprae," over a century ago, but its method of transmission is still not clear. What is clear, as indicated, is that the disease is not easily spread; it is far less contagious than originally assumed. Many people live in close proximity to sufferers from Hansen's disease, and never become infected. The disease has been known for centuries, and has never achieved pandemic status. In fact most human beings, some 95%, appear not to be susceptible to it at all.[7]

It requires no conversations with any of the few remaining residents in Kalaupapa to appreciate how forcible separation from home, community, and loved ones damaged those who were its victims. The National Park Service makes available (Note: it sometimes requires persistence to retrieve it) an undated report, "Leprosy in Hawaii," describing the damage. "For the benefit of the healthy, persons suspected of leprosy were condemned to a life of virtual imprisonment on the windward side of the island of Moloka'i. The concept of segregation was completely alien to the fundamentals of Hawai'ian society and therefore greatly resented." The report notes that many people questioned whether the disease was even contagious, and that the Board's actions in any case "were seen a penalties upon individuals afflicted by something beyond their control." The result was a "mass psychological deterioration" in the community that was detrimental to the culture as a whole. "The energetic pursuit of sick individuals was a great blow to their friends and relatives. The high degree of sociability among Hawai'ians more or less preordained that those banished to Moloka'i would be doomed to lives of despair." It should therefore be expected to read that "parents refused to let their children go, husbands and wives resisted separation, and old people implored to live out their days where they had spent their lives. Many took refuge in the countryside in ravines and caves or homes of friends, where they were sought after by the police who had been empowered by the Board of Health to seek out the unfortunates. Victims and their family and friends resorted to violence against the authorities," who eventually used violence in return. At the "end of 1866, more than one hundred victims were driven on board ship," and "descriptions of the departure of the victims are heart-rending to read."[8]

Also heart-rending to read is the autobiography, or memoir, by Olivia Robello Breitha, *Olivia: My Life of Exile in Kalaupapa*. In a literary equivalent of folk art, she pours out her feelings. She was seventeen when a "bounty hunter" in 1934 ordered her to report to the Board of Health.[9] Eventually, in 1937, the territorial government exiled her to Kalaupapa. Although sulfone drugs were discovered to cure Hansen's disease in the early 1940s, it was not until 1969 that she, and the other former patients, was free to leave. Only then were the laws mandating exile for sufferers of the disease rescinded. Note that at this time Hawaii had been a state for more than a decade. Discovering that she had no more life on the outside, she ultimately returned to Kalaupapa, as did a number of other former patients. The state then provided for them there, and continues to do so. Breitha died at the age of 90, in 2006.[10]

Fewer than three dozen former patients now reside in Kalaupapa. After they are gone, the site will become a park. In the meantime, access is rigidly controlled to protect the privacy of the residents. Except for tightly-regimented tours that the community conducts, no outsiders are permitted unless they are there by invitation from a resident. Upon landing at the small airport, visitors are warned not to leave the premises unless accompanied by an official. Those who are permitted to visit may take photographs, but not of residents without their express permission. Their desire for privacy is strong, and understandable. Throughout Hawaii, there are now about twenty cases of Hansen's disease treated each year. Those infected now are treated as outpatients.[11]

The Kalaupapa experience with regard to American hysteria over Hansen's disease was not unique, only the most dramatic. The USA reacted similarly on the mainland, banishing victims to a colony, Carville, in Louisiana. A release from the Smithsonian's National Museum of American History described it as follows:

On the United States mainland, the response to leprosy had national implications; in 1921 the federal government purchased the Louisiana Leper Home as a national center for disease containment and isolated care. The instatement of the Federal Marine Hospital #66, a national leprosarium, was unique. The government, under the auspices of the Public Health Service, assumed extensive financial and administrative responsibility to create an institution devoted solely to leprosy's treatment and containment for the entire continental United States. Only within the last 20 years has Washington returned the Carville center to the State of Louisiana and relocated its research branch—The Gillis W. Long Hansen's Disease Center—to Baton Rouge, Louisiana.[12]

Whether quarantine could ever be completely effective on a mass scale for influenza is doubtful, because of the extraordinarily contagious nature of the disease. Of course it can succeed in localities if applied rigorously and sufficiently early to achieve complete isolation. During the 1918 pandemic, Gunnison, Colorado "succeeded in isolating itself. So did Fairbanks, Alaska. American Samoa escaped without a single case, while a few miles away in Western Samoa, 22 percent of the entire population died." An Army study found that most efforts were "carelessly applied," and therefore failed, but that isolation "rigidly applied...did some good."[13]

For Hansen's disease, the situation is different and would appear to be more promising; quarantine might appear to be effective. Nevertheless, it was never fully effective in Hawaii. The long incubation period and the strong resistance of the population to the laws mandating exile worked against its success.

"THE MAGIC OF THE MARKETPLACE" AND PUBLIC HEALTH EMERGENCIES

An example of inaction in the face of a public health emergency may be seen in the case of the Eisenhower administration regarding the impending pandemic of "Asian flu," in 1957. The cause was a new virus that had been identified in Asia early in the year, and had been circulating in the USA "as early as June—months before the pandemic mortality impact began."[14] If the volume of relevant material at the Eisenhower Presidential Library is any indication, Asian flu was not a major issue of Eisenhower's administration. The Library's collection has only forty-five pages of material, many of them duplicates or near duplicates.

On 17 August 1957, an attorney in the Bronx, Robert Himmelfarb, sent a handwritten letter to the president expressing alarm that only six companies would be producing vaccine. "It is respectfully asked that this should be increased to combat the expected flu epidemic," he wrote, and mentioned an article in that day's *New York Times*.[15] The response to Himmelfarb went out on 5 September over the signature of Eisenhower's physician, Major General Howard Snyder, who indicated that President Eisenhower had asked him to reply. "The United States Public Health Service has set up a well-organized plan for the manufacture and distribution of the Asian flu vaccine," he wrote. "Everything possible is being done to have sufficient vaccine available to everyone at the earliest possible date."[16]

A "Special Staff Note" with Eisenhower's initials, dated October 3, 1957, and marked "Administratively Confidential" indicated that the "Public Health Service has taken all reasonable precautionary steps in preparation for the anticipated epidemics in collaboration with the AMA, state health officers, the drug industry, and others concerned." At the time, it said, there were an estimated 225,650 cases reported throughout the country. "It is approaching epidemic proportions in Louisiana, Mississippi, Arizona, eastern Texas, Utah and possibly other areas." Vaccine supplies "sufficient to inoculate first-priority groups" were expected within "the next few weeks." The military had 62% of the vaccine required for first inoculation of all active-duty personnel, and defense agencies had been directed to "assist in establishing vaccination programs for civilian employees as supplies become available." The key provision regarding the policy was the statement that "vaccine manufacturers have agreed to voluntary distribution among States according to population, and have been asked to follow the priority recommendations of State and local advisory committees in filling orders. This voluntary type of distribution system cannot be expected to be uniformly effective, but more stringent controls are not recommended at this time."[17]

Governor Albert Chandler of Kentucky on 24 October 1957 sent an urgent telegram to Eisenhower, indicating that Asian flu had reached epidemic proportions in Pike County, and that vaccine was unavailable. He asked the president to intervene. The reply had originally been drafted for the signature of Eisenhower's chief of staff, Sherman Adams, but ultimately the signature was that of Howard Pyle, deputy assistant for federal state relations. The reply indicated that Kentucky was receiving the amount "of the scarce vaccine" allotted by the manufacturers, who distributed it on the basis of population. "Since influenza has reached epidemic stage in many areas throughout United States [*sic*], intervention by Federal Government to secure additional supplies for one area could seriously and unfairly affect others. It is suggested that you or your State health officer request the Kentucky outlets of the vaccine manufacturers to give special attention to filling orders for Pike County from Kentucky's share of new vaccine supplies."[18]

According to Mike Davis, public health experts appealed to the Eisenhower administration for a mass vaccination program, but the administration "rebuffed" them. The surgeon general did provide some funds for surveillance, but (as the records clearly verify) "the Republicans in power relied upon free enterprise to develop and distribute the vaccine." This obviously was inadequate, as Snyder's reference to "the scarce vaccine" demonstrates. Davis noted scathingly that contrary to the administration's assumptions, "without government coordination classical supply-and-demand relationships work mischievously" when influenza is involved. Timing is among the difficulties. "The vaccine needs to be produced in quantity for immunization at least a month before the peak of an epidemic, but most of the market demand from individual consumers comes only after the epidemic is in full course." Even though by 1957 there was a considerable range of antibiotics to treat secondary infections, and even though Asian flu rarely produced viral pneumonia, cyanosis, and acute respiratory distress and thus was far less lethal than its 1918 predecessor, "still, 2 million people worldwide were later estimated to have perished in the pandemic, including 80,000 Americans, many of whom might have been saved by timely vaccination."[19] This is speculation, of course, but it is plausible.

Davis went on to cite the opinion of "public-health veterans" that "these deaths were the dismal price of the failure of Eisenhower's reliance upon the invisible hand of private enterprise to do the work of government," and he agrees fully with Millar and Osborne that dependence upon the "profit-driven vaccine marketplace" with all its inefficiencies caused a huge and unnecessary loss of life. Among those inefficiencies are inadequate levels of production, and diversion of vaccine away from high-risk groups and to corporate employees in order to reduce sick days.[20]

MILITANT PASSIVITY FROM THE LEFT HAND, AUTHORITARIANISM FROM THE RIGHT

It might appear as if the two extremes of inappropriate governmental responses to public health emergencies would be over-reaction—as in the case of Hawaii and Hansen's disease—and inaction—as in the case of Eisenhower's passivity when Asian flu confronted the country. Unfortunately, the range is even greater. Beyond simple inaction there is an example of an even more extreme response, one that could even be termed militant passivity. In the face of the most lethal pandemic in modern history, President Woodrow Wilson not only remained inactive but took other actions that (unintentionally, of course, even if not necessarily unknowingly) made matters far worse.

Wilson had strongly resisted entry into the World War, and in fact achieved his narrow re-election in 1916 campaigning on the slogan, "He Kept us Out of War!" When he reluctantly concluded that the USA must participate, however, he passionately marshaled the country's resources to throw into the war effort, and discarded many of the restraints on government that had characterized America since its beginning. Barry's description of wartime America under Wilson is chilling, and parallels the picture that Katherine Anne Porter presented so subtly, yet forcefully, in *Pale Horse, Pale Rider.*

The country was ill-prepared when it entered the fray in April of 1917, but hardly more than a year later "Wilson had injected the government into every facet of national life and had created great bureaucratic engines to focus all the nation's attention and intent on the war."[21] America, Barry continued, found its food supply under the control of a Food Administration, a Fuel Administration rationing its gasoline and coal, and "a War Industries Board to oversee the entire economy." Wilson controlled the railroads and many industries.

Most disturbing from the standpoint of civil liberties, "he created a vast propaganda machine, an internal spy network, a bond-selling apparatus extending to the level of residential city blocks. He had even succeeded in stifling speech, in the summer of 1918 arresting and imprisoning— some for prison terms longer than ten years—not just radical labor leaders and editors of German-language newspapers but powerful men, even a congressman."[22] The "internal spy network" was the American Protective League mentioned in Chapter II (p. 21). A look at the Duluth, Minnesota chapter will provide some sense of its activities.

A history of Duluth and St. Louis County says that the "local unit of the APL had seven divisions, each of which had 'a captain and a lieutenant, and these were the only persons in each division who knew the Chief's identity, he being known as C-1.' Continuing the clandestine pattern, division leaders also were kept uninformed as to the identities of personnel and leaders of other divisions. It seems to have worked... 'The Department of Justice today [1921] has a complete record of every person living in the Duluth area who uttered words against the Government from April 1, 1917, until the Duluth division was disbanded under Federal instructions on February 1, 1919." The Duluth unit received praise for clearing up "more cases of pro-Germanism and sedition," and for causing the "greatest number of arrests and detention."[23]

One person Wilson dared not touch spoke out forcefully against the repression, and almost assuredly kept it from becoming even worse. Wilson's nemesis, former president Theodore Roosevelt, condemned the administration's excesses, and dared Wilson to have him arrested. Kathleen Dalton's superb study of Roosevelt details this almost completely overlooked role that the former president played in a time of national hysteria. Most treatments of Roosevelt's activities during the Great War condemn him as acting irresponsibly. Dalton helps to correct this myopic view. She points out that "*The Nation* asked 'Why is Roosevelt Unjailed?' in an editorial criticizing the administration's bad habit of jailing less famous adversaries. The editorial credited the ex-president with having saved the right of free speech in wartime."[24] To be sure, Theodore Roosevelt was no absolutist on civil liberties—and certainly not on free speech in wartime—but it is inexcusable that most works dealing with his post-presidential public career tend to treat him solely as a pugnacious militarist, and ignore his role in opposing repressive government.

From the point of view of public health, the most disturbing were some of Wilson's other actions. As is customary during military mobilization, dozens of military installations sprang up, and each one increasingly concentrated thousands of personnel into a crowded area. Wilson "had injected the government into American life in ways unlike any other in the nation's history. And the final extension of federal power had come only in the spring of 1918, after the first wave of influenza had begun jumping from camp to camp, when the government expanded the draft from males between the ages of twenty-one and thirty to those between the ages of eighteen and forty-five."[25]

During this time, disagreements between the War Department and the Army's Medical Department brought turmoil in the midst of the pandemic. William Gorgas, the Army's surgeon general, annoyed Secretary of

War Newton Baker and Army Chief of Staff Peyton March with, among other things, his demands for measures to combat influenza's spread. March and Baker forced Gorgas into retirement, thus dealing a blow to the Medical Department at a time when it was most needed.

Gorgas's interim replacement, Brigadier General Charles Richard, also spoke up; he warned of the dangers of continuing to ship men to Europe aboard crowded transports, while General John J. Pershing in France—who pointed out that receiving men who were ill was counterproductive—called for more medical personnel and hospital space aboard ships, and a one-week quarantine of troops before shipping. General March, however (who, as the Army's chief of staff, of course was not a physician), insisted that a physical examination of each soldier being sent to board ship would be sufficient. He ignored, or dismissed, General Richard's assertion that no physical examination could identify those who were infected, but who had not yet displayed symptoms.[26]

President Wilson was concerned, to be sure, and called March to a meeting at the White House. At this time, in October, peace already appeared to be at hand, and the carnage from the flu was clearly evident. Crosby cites one incident prior to the meeting in which a convoy arrived in France with 24,488 men, of whom 4,147 were ill upon arrival, 1,357 required hospitalization immediately, and more than 200 had died.[27]

Wilson indicated that he had been advised to halt the shipment of men abroad until the epidemic had passed, but March said that the shipments should continue. He pointed out that the men were subject to examination at their training camps, at their embarkation camps, and again before boarding ship. He conceded that epidemics on ship could still occur, but that "lives lost to influenza must be balanced against those which could be saved if the war could be brought to a speedy end."[28] In his opinion, no other circumstance was sufficient to justify halting the shipment of troops.

Crosby's discussion quoted March as writing later that, after making the decision to continue troop shipment, Wilson looked sadly out the window, and said, "General, I wonder if you have heard this limerick?

I had a little bird
And its name was Enza...

This, if true, is a damning indictment. Wilson appears to have had at least some idea of what the consequences would be. As a result of his decision, one of the military's greatest shortages came to be coffins for its troops who had succumbed on the voyage abroad or soon after. Pershing, himself, later implied that War Department policies promoted the pandemic, because "large numbers of cases were brought in by our troop ships."[29]

However much Wilson exercised power during the war, he exerted no power to deal with influenza, either among the troops or among the civilian population. To be sure, there was little medically that could be done at the time (even now, our therapeutic resources are limited), but avoiding overcrowded conditions, providing adequate nursing care, and perhaps even implementing quarantine under some conditions might have assisted somewhat.

Kalaupapa resulted from an over-reaction—possibly a hysterical one—because of ignorance. Eisenhower's response to the Asian flu pandemic resulted from adherence to a free-market ideology that was inadequate to deal with the situation. Wilson's response to the greatest threat of all, the 1918 flu, resulted from a single-minded preoccupation with the war that clouded his judgment. His zeal prevented him (and his key military adviser, General March) from recognizing that accepting additional influenza deaths by continuing troop shipments was actually detrimental to their war efforts.

IDEOLOGY, INCOMPETENCE, BUT SOME THOUGHTFUL PLANNING

There is yet another category of misguided response to public health crises, one that combines several of the reasons above—especially ignorance and ideology—and couples them to inadequate infrastructure, sheer incompetence of officials at the highest levels, and what seemed to many observers, however unkindly, even to be a lack of concern. This was the response of the George W. Bush administration to the disaster of Hurricane Katrina in 2005. To be sure, this was not a pandemic, but much can be learned from the government's clumsy response of things to be avoided when faced with any public health emergency, pandemics included.

Note, though, that this is not the complete story with regard to the Bush administration. It performed considerably better with regard to preparation for pandemic influenza. Regardless of whether its Katrina experience was instructive, the Bush administration's pandemic flu preparation was largely unheralded, probably because the country did not seem actually to be facing a pandemic at the time. Bush should receive some credit for a non-dramatic success, just as it received blame for a very dramatic failure regarding Katrina. In this instance, it appears as though his guidance came from experts in public health and related fields, with minimal influence from ideology.

On 1 November 2005, Bush announced his program of preparation, and later, in May of 2006, released *National Strategy for Pandemic Influenza: Implementation Plan*.[30] In Bush's introduction, he said that Congress in December had appropriated $3.8 billion, and that he had launched the International Partnership for Avian and Pandemic Influenza at the UN the previous September. The plan, he said, "describes more than 300 critical actions, many of which have already been initiated, to address the threat of pandemic influenza." He spoke of the need for participation of "all levels of government and segments of society." The nine chapters of the plan included a summary, two chapters on government planning and response, two on "international efforts and transportation and borders," one on "Protecting Human Health," another on "Protecting Animal Health," one on "Law Enforcement, Public Safety, and Security," and a final one on institutional considerations, such as "plans by Federal, State, local, and tribal authorities, businesses, schools, and non-governmental organizations to ensure continuity of operations and maintenance of critical infrastructure."

Without acknowledging the two previous presidents (both Republicans) with relevant experience, but perhaps in consideration of lessons learned from the Eisenhower and Ford administrations, the Bush plan summarized its call for production, stockpiling, and distribution of vaccine and antiviral medications:

Achieving National Goals for Production and Stockpiling of Vaccine and Antiviral Medications
The Federal Government has established two primary vaccine goals (1) establishment and maintenance of stockpiles of pre-pandemic vaccine adequate to immunize 20 million persons against influenza strains that present a pandemic threat; and (2) expansion of domestic influenza vaccine manufacturing surge capacity for the production of pandemic vaccines for the entire domestic population within 6 months of a pandemic declaration. The Federal Government has also established two primary goals for stockpiling existing antiviral medications: (1) establishment and maintenance of stockpiles adequate to treat 75 million persons, divided between Federal and State stockpiles; and (2) establishment and maintenance of a Federal stockpile of 6 million treatment courses reserved for domestic containment efforts.

To accomplish these goals, we will expand Federal, and create State, stockpiles of influenza countermeasures, as well as expand domestic vaccine manufacturing capacity. We will make substantial new investments in the advanced development of cell-culture-based influenza vaccine candidates, with a goal of establishing the domestic surge vaccine production capacity to meet our pre-pandemic stockpile and post-pandemic vaccine production goals.

Prioritizing and Distributing Limited Supplies of Vaccine and Antiviral Medications
The Federal Government is developing guidelines to assist State, local, and tribal governments and the private sector in defining groups that should receive priority access to existing limited supplies of vaccine and antiviral medications. Priority recommendations will reflect the pandemic response goals of limiting mortality and severe morbidity; maintaining critical infrastructure and societal function; diminishing economic impacts; and maintaining national security. Priorities for vaccine and antiviral drug use will vary based on pandemic severity as well as the vaccine and drug supply.

The establishment of credible distribution plans for our countermeasures is equally important. We will work with State and tribal entities to develop and exercise influenza countermeasure distribution plans, to include the necessary logistical support of such plans, including security provisions.[31]

It was Katrina, however, that showed the Bush administration at its worst in terms of efficiency and effectiveness. The infrastructure was inadequate, and was weakened further by an ideology of "privatization." In this instance, modern media coverage was so pervasive that contemporary America saw clearly the results of a government controlled by overly ideological officials who in any case gave the impression of being uncaring and unqualified to deal with the disaster—regardless of whether they were so inclined. Many Americans remember the spectacle of their president, the younger Bush, viewing the destruction from the air as he passed over the stricken city. The spectacle continued. More than two years after the storm, much expensive equipment designated for housing and restoration sat unused and deteriorating, while in February 2008 news outlets around the country reported that thousands of people who had been living in many of the trailers and manufactured houses that FEMA had purchased for nearly $1 billion were being told to leave quickly, because their shelters exposed them to toxic levels of formaldehyde, a carcinogen. Even later, in March, the Associated Press reported that "years after Hurricane Katrina, tens of thousands of miserable homeowners are still waiting for their government rebuilding checks, and many complain they can't even get their calls returned." To be sure, not everyone suffered: "The company that holds the big contract to distribute that aid, however, is doing quite well for itself," a news item said. "ICF International of Fairfax, Va, has posted strong profits, gone public, landed additional multimillion dollar government contracts, and, it was learned this week, secured a potentially big raise recently from the state of Louisiana."[32]

Historian Douglas Brinkley, who lived in New Orleans at the time of the hurricane, produced a powerful work on Katrina, the circumstances leading up to the catastrophe, and the Bush administration's failed response.[33] There have been many other comments on presidential actions and the politics of Katrina, but those that may be especially helpful in considering presidential responses to health-care disasters are a thoughtful essay in *The New Yorker* by David Remnick[34] and my own examination of presidential reactions to disasters in general, in *The Journal of Risk, Hazards, and Crisis in Public Policy*.[35]

In addition to his book, Brinkley also wrote a powerful op-ed article for *The Washington Post*. The title was bitter, and appropriate: "Reckless Abandonment." In this piece, Brinkley pointed out that "two full years after the hurricane, the Big Easy is barely limping along," and all the "most important issues concerning the city's long-term survival are still up in the air."[36] Despite "billion-dollar band aids," he said, White House directives are "placebos." He pointed out that inaction, itself, can and often does result from a deliberate policy decision. Almost the only people working to restore the city at that time were volunteers, and they tended ultimately to become cynical, disillusioned, and exhausted from their efforts. "Katrina," Brinkley wrote, "exposed all the ills of urban America— endemic poverty, institutionalized racism, failing public schools and much more. New Orleans," he said, "is just a microcosm…" America is faced with a decision, and that is whether "the current policy of inaction is really the way we want to deal with the worst natural disaster in our history."

Fortunately, America's responses to public health emergencies have not always been misguided. Some have been excellent, and others have been better than generally supposed.

Notes

1. For a timeline, see "History of Quarantine," *The Most Dangerous Woman in America.* Nova website, 2004; http://www.pbs.org/wgbh/nova/typhoid/quarantine.html; retrieved 8 June 2015.
2. Dylan Tierney, MD and Edward A. Nardell, MD, "Leprosy," *Merck Manual* (February 2014) http://www.merck.com/mmhe/sec17/ch194/ch194a.html; retrieved 8 June 2015.
3. *Ibid.*
4. Jack London, "The Lepers of Molokai," *Woman's Home Companion* (January 1908); available at http://carl-bell.baylor.edu/JL/TheLepersOfMolokai.html; retrieved 9 June 2015.
5. Olivia Robello Breitha, *Olivia: My Life of Exile in Kalaupapa,* 2nd printing. Honolulu: Arizona Memorial Association, 2003; this was verified by my discussions on Moloka'I and in Kalaupapa during the period of 3–10 March 2007. Considerations of privacy precluded photographs of discussants, recordings, notes, or attribution—all comments off the record; cited hereafter (with permission) as "Discussions."
6. London, p. 3.
7. Tierney and Nardell.
8. "Leprosy in Hawaii," undated, typescript from National Park Service http://www.nps.gov/parkhistory/online_books/kala/pdf/B3LepHawaii.pdf; retrieved 9 June 2015.
9. Breitha, p. 8.
10. See Taylor Maurand, "Feeling Out Leprosy," *Hypercube,* Center for Science and Medical Journalism, Boston University College of Communication (3 November); http://www.bu.edu/phpbin/news-cms/news/?dept=1127&id=41520; retrieved 14 June 2015.
11. *Ibid.*
12. NMAH, "Oh Say Can you See: Stories from the National Museum of American History," Smithsonian Institution (16 August 2011); http://americanhistory.si.edu/blog/2011/08/the-history-of-leprosy.html; retrieved 16 July 2015.
13. John M. Barry, "1918 Revisited: Lessons and Suggestions for Further Inquiry." *The Threat of Pandemic Influenza: Workshop Summary.* Washington: National Academies Press Institute of Medicine, 2005, pp. 62–63.
14. L. Simonsen, et al., "Pandemic Influenza and Mortality: Past Evidence and Projections for the Future," *The Threat of Pandemic Influenza,* Washington: National Academies Press (Institute of Medicine), 2005, p. 105.
15. Robert Himmelfarb, "Letter to President Eisenhower" (19 August 1957), Eisenhower Presidential Library, Records as President, White House Central Files, Official File Box 606 OF 117-T Asian Influenza.

16. Howard, Snyder, "Letter to Robert Himmelfarb" (5 September 1957), Eisenhower Presidential Library, Records as President, White House Central Files, Official File Box 606 OF 117-T Asian Influenza.
17. "Special Staff Note" (3 October 1957), Dwight D. Eisenhower Papers as President, DDE Diary Series, Box 27 Toner Notes October.
18. Howard Pyle to Albert Chandler (25 October 1957), Eisenhower Presidential Library, Records as President, White House Central Files, Official File Box 606 OF 117-T Asian Influenza.
19. Mike, Davis, 2006. *The Monster at Our Door: The Global Threat of Avian Flu*. New York: Henry Holt, 2006, pp. 35–36.
20. J. Donald Millar, and June Osborne, "Precursors of the Scientific Decision-Making Process Leading to the 1976 National Immunization Campaign," in *Influenza in America: 1918–1976*, June Osborne, ed. New York: Prodist, 1977, pp. 19–22.
21. Barry, p. 300.
22. *Ibid.*, pp. 300–301.
23. Max J. Skidmore, *Moose Crossing: Portland to Portland on the Theodore Roosevelt International Highway*, Lanham, Maryland: Hamilton Books, 2007, p. 106.
24. Kathleen Dalton, *Theodore Roosevelt: A Strenuous Life*. New York: Alfred A. Knopf, 2002, p. 490.
25. Barry, p. 301.
26. Carol R. Byerly, *Fever of War: The Influenza Epidemic in the U.S. Army during World War I*, New York: New York University Press, 2005, pp. 104–106.
27. Alfred W. Crosby, *America's Forgotten Pandemic: The Influenza of 1918*. Cambridge, England: Cambridge University Press, 2003, p. 124.
28. *Ibid.*, p. 125.
29. Byerly, p. 108.
30. Homeland Security Council, *National Strategy for Pandemic Influenza: Implementation Plan*, May 2006.
31. *Ibid.*, p. 9.
32. "Survivors of Katrina Wait for Aid," *Kansas City Star* (14 March 2008), pp. A1 ff.
33. Douglas Brinkley, *The Great Deluge: Hurricane Katrina, New Orleans, and the Mississippi Gulf Coast*. New York: Harper Perennial, 2007.
34. David Remnick, "Letter from Louisiana: High Water: How Presidents and Citizens React to Disaster," *The New Yorker* (3 October 2005).
35. Max J. Skidmore, "Anti-Government is Not the Solution to Our Problem, Anti-Government IS the Problem: Presidential Response to Natural Disasters, San Francisco to Katrina," *Journal of Risk, Hazards, and Crisis in Public Policy* 4:1 (March 2013).
36. Douglas Brinkley, "Reckless Abandonment." *The Washington Post* (26 August 2007).

CHAPTER 4

Appropriate Responses to Public Health Emergencies

Abstract Happily, there are also many examples of sound responses to public health emergencies, pandemic or otherwise. A notable example was that of President Theodore Roosevelt's immediate and effective response to the San Francisco earthquake of 1906. This involved close coordination of private resources along with massive aid from the Departments of War and Navy, using army and naval troops and resources.

President Lyndon Johnson's response to Hurricane Betsy, also in New Orleans, is another stellar example, as was his response to the great Alaskan earthquake of 1964. These demonstrate that quick and effective government action is indeed possible. It requires leaders who determine to make government operate well, and who know how to do it.

Such leaders, of course, must believe that good government is possible. It is unreasonable to expect that elected officials who simply do not believe in government could ever make one work well.

Keywords Katrina • Lyndon Johnson • G.W. Bush administration • Effective public administration • Theodore Roosevelt • Hurricane Betsy • Alaska Earthquake • San Francisco Earthquake

© The Author(s) 2016
M.J. Skidmore, *Presidents, Pandemics, and Politics*, The Evolving American Presidency, DOI 10.1057/978-1-137-59959-9_4

43

Fortunately, the responses to emergencies discussed in the previous chapter do not form the complete record. There are also more favorable examples of executive reactions to public health emergencies. One of these—certainly not a pandemic but instructive nonetheless because it demonstrates that well-crafted government response can be effective against an enormous public health crisis even with early twentieth-century technology—was the San Francisco earthquake.

PRESIDENTIAL ACTION AND THE SAN FRANCISCO EARTHQUAKE

On 18 April 1906, a huge earthquake struck San Francisco, causing widespread fires to follow. The destruction both from shaking and from fire was extraordinary.[1] Gas from ruptured mains fed the fires, and broken water pipes made it impossible to get them under control. According to the U. S. Geological Survey, the event "ranks as one of the most significant earthquakes of all time."[2] The U. S. Census Bureau reported that the series of "catastrophic fires...burned for three days and destroyed more than 500 blocks in the heart of the city." The death toll, according to conservative estimates, was more than 3,000, "with some estimates as high as 6,000." Property damage in today's dollars amounted to about $8.2 billion, and "between 225,000 and 300,000 people were left homeless." This was the major part of San Francisco's total population, which in 1900 was 342,782.[3] The city at the time of the quake was roughly the size that New Orleans had become nearly a century later in August 2005, when Hurricane Katrina slammed into that other uniquely American treasure. In 1906, though, the conditions were far different, and that was fortunate for San Francisco. Government rushed to help, and did so effectively, making the outcome vastly more favorable for San Francisco than it was for New Orleans a century later.

The president at the time was arguably the most active and vigorous president in American history, Theodore Roosevelt. Rather than sit back and observe passively, or making a half-hearted effort with public relations uppermost in mind, he immediately marshaled the full force of the national government. He even sent a full cabinet secretary to San Francisco, Victor H. Metcalf, who headed the Department of Commerce and Labor. Metcalf was not only to represent the president personally but also to be his eyes and ears on the scene. Shortly after arriving Metcalf had completed a study of the situation, and sent his findings in a long telegram to the president. This was only the first of such reports.[4]

In the meantime, another cabinet secretary, Secretary of War (and future president) William Howard Taft, was busy sending trains loaded with relief supplies and assorted equipment. Taft also sought his own sources of information, and wired the local military command ordering them to supply it.[5] Taft, in addition, ordered the army to supply all necessary assistance possible. The commanding general at Vancouver Barracks, Washington, received a telegram from the Army chief of staff, to the effect that: "Secretary of War directs you have Commissary...send two hundred thousand rations to Depot Commissary, San Francisco; also all available hospital, wall and conical wall tents to depot quartermaster, with least delay possible, by quickest practicable route either by water or rail," and directed further: "Acknowledge receipt and report action."[6]

The War Department also telegraphed the commanding general in San Francisco to report how many "troops from outside" his division he needed, and noted significantly: "In assisting stricken people War Department is agreeable to any reasonable plans and requests of the properly constituted civil authorities, but return to normal conditions should be as rapid as practicable. There is no law for such use of the Army, and it is desired to avoid sending additional troops from elsewhere if possible. All available tentage in possession of Army now in or on way to San Francisco."[7] This is especially important, in that the government was acting in the absence of any formal authority to deal with a dire emergency. Furthermore, "until the establishment of the various city hospitals all civilian patients were admitted without charge."[8]

The people of San Francisco were grateful, and the local news media praised the government. The *San Francisco Chronicle* headline on 3 May said, "Great Work by Signal Corps: Lines are run over Ruined Walls and Through Smoking Streets During Fire."[9] A prominent national magazine ran an article in July by the local commanding general, "How the Army Worked to Save San Francisco," gushing, "How lucky it was for San Francisco that Gen. Frederick Funston threw himself and his men so boldly into the breach when the fire-fighters were waging their unequal combat with the flames..."[10] The magazine was *Cosmopolitan*, which obviously was a considerably different journal then.

The Navy also worked diligently to provide relief, sending the U.S.S. "Boston" filled with relief supplies, as well as personnel to help.[11] Gladys Hansen, of the San Francisco Museum, has reported that a classified Navy document was made available in the 1980s. It is an "extraordinary report of Lieutenant Frederick Freeman" that was discovered in the national Archives at San Bruno. The report "details the superb work of the U. S. Navy in rescue and firefighting work during the Great Earthquake and Fire." The immediate question would be why it was ever classified to begin with, and Hansen admitted, "there is some mystery as to why this document was classified by the Navy," but she supplied the answer. Careful reading, she said, "clearly shows that Gen. Funston usurped local civilian authority. He essentially ran the fire suppression activities like a military campaign. With civilian authority in such disarray, as outlined in this report, the better-equipped military filled the vacuum." The important thing is that it worked.

Difficulties certainly remained; it would be unrealistic to have expected everything to go well, but San Francisco—aided considerably by the US Government—pulled itself together, and came back. In many ways the rebuilt city was better than it had been before the earthquake. The transportation system was again operating, with trams running on regular schedules. Banks were not only open but were operating vigorously. They quickly began clearing more money than previously, and in fact more than in any other western city. There were funds for those in need. "Homeless families were housed in temporary wooden cottages in city parks. There was plenty of food." Unions supplied workers to rebuild structures that had been destroyed, and the city succeeded in building 20,000 new permanent buildings in only three years. Nine years after the devastation of the great quake, in 1915 "San Francisco threw a world's fair."[12]

In the aftermath of Katrina, *Business Week* published a thoughtful article that looked back at the San Francisco destruction, and suggested that there were lessons to be learned from that century-old disaster, lessons that should have been helpful in reconstructing New Orleans.[13] It is unclear whether anyone in the Bush administration read the article. What is clear is that there is no one in Washington who gave any indication of having paid attention to *Business Week*'s suggestions, to the San Francisco experience, or to any expert opinion that could have been helpful. What America succeeded in doing in 1906, saving one of its premier cities, it failed to do a century later in 2005.

PRESIDENTIAL ACTION AND HURRICANE BETSY

Hurricane Katrina, of course, was not New Orleans's first experience with a severe hurricane. It is instructive to view the experience of the city, four decades earlier, when on 9 September 1965, Hurricane Betsy, another powerful storm, pounded New Orleans. The power of the two storms was not equal, but the destruction that they wrought was similar. The outcomes were what were far different. When Betsy created its victims, those victims had a major resource denied the victims of Katrina: Lyndon B. Johnson as the sitting president. Not only did he have confidence in government, he knew how to make it work. Moreover, he cared.

Shortly after the Hurricane, President Lyndon Johnson was on the telephone to Buford Ellington, his director of emergency planning. He said of the people of Louisiana: "I want them to know they're loved." Just after 5:00 that afternoon of the 10th, Air Force One, bearing LBJ, was in the air on its way toward New Orleans. After landing, with no power for loudspeakers, Johnson shouted, over a 25-mph wind, words that reporter Brian Williams remarked, "bordered on the poetic." He had rushed to New Orleans, LBJ said, "because I wanted to see with my own eyes what the unhappy alliance of wind and water have done to this land and its people."[14]

Johnson assured the people that their troubles became his first priority:

Today at 3 o'clock when Senator Long and Congressman Boggs and Congressman Willis called me on behalf of the entire Louisiana delegation, I put aside all the problems on my desk to come to Louisiana as soon as I could. I have observed from flying over your city how great the catastrophe is that you have experienced. Human suffering and physical damage are measureless. I'm here this evening to pledge to you the full resources of the federal government to Louisiana to help repair as best we can the injury that has been done by nature.

Throughout the day I have talked to Senator Long and Senator Ellender, Congressmen Boggs and Willis, my friend Jimmy Morrison, Otto Passman and Congressman Wagner about what has taken place in this great state. As we flew to New Orleans we discussed the ways and means of putting the compassion of the United States in specific and helpful action. With me are Governor Buford Ellington, in charge of the federal government's Office of Emergency Planning, and whose responsibility it is to make sure that all needs to be done gets done and quickly as possible. Also with me are Secretary of Agriculture Orville Freeman, General Collins, Chairman of the American Red Cross, Dr. Luther Terry, the Surgeon General of the United States. Mr. -- the head of our Small Business Administration is here, and we'll have further announcements as we go along. Mr. Gene Foley will have a briefing just before we return to Washington on what that agency will be able to do.

Throughout the day I have talked to Senator Long and Senator Ellender,
The agony and the loss of Louisiana would have been far greater without the cooperation, effective work of the Weather Bureau, the Civil Defense Authorities of Louisiana, the Red Cross and other local groups.

I'm delighted to see your mayor has been on the job for many hours now and is here to welcome us. More than 180,000 citizens were evacuated from southern Louisiana alone. Because we were alerted to the assault of Hurricane Betsy, I am ordering in teams from the Office of Emergency Planning, the Army Corps of Engineers immediately. The Small Business Administration has already declared this area a disaster area and will be prepared to make long-term loans to rehabilitate both business establishments and all the homes that we saw, their roofs under water a few moments ago.[15]

Then President Johnson and his party drove into the city. Along the way, he heard cries of "water, water." LBJ took immediate action, making sure that water was delivered and given to those in need. Those were days before bottled water was generally available, so LBJ arranged for soft drink manufacturers to supply it.[16]

"Hurricane Katrina was more devastating than Betsy," to be sure, but Betsy also caused widespread destruction, and LBJ's government responded to Betsy quickly and effectively. "L.B.J. and the local officials of New Orleans and the State of Louisiana responded to their crisis with far greater coordination and speed than their successors in 2005." Nevertheless, there were dire rumors; in both instances, many people believed that white elites deliberately protected their areas, while leaving black sections to the floods.[17] Despite the rumors, Johnson's commanding presence was vital. That, and his insistence on following through, made an enormous difference. Many accounts tell of LBJ's interactions with the stricken. Often they are sanitized, but over and over people mentioned an incident that James Lee Burke included in his powerful post-Katrina novel *The Tin Roof Blowdown*. The sheriff was speaking to the novel's protagonist, Deputy Dave Robicheaux:

"What did you think of Lyndon Johnson?" she asked.

"Before or after I got to Vietnam?"

"When Hurricane Betsy hit New Orleans in '65, Johnson flew into town and went to a shelter full of people who had been evacuated from Algiers. It was dark inside and people were scared and didn't know what was going to happen to them. He shined a flashlight in his face and said, 'My name is Lyndon Baines Johnson. I'm your goddamn president and I'm here to tell you my office and the people of the United States are behind you.' Not bad, huh?"[18]

PRESIDENTIAL ACTION AND THE ALASKAN EARTHQUAKE

Johnson's response to Hurricane Betsy was characteristic, and was not an isolated incident. He had responded immediately and effectively the year before Hurricane Betsy hit New Orleans, when a monster earthquake hit Alaska. It was "the largest ever recorded in North America in terms of magnitude," although the "1906 San Francisco earthquake was the worst U.S. earthquake in terms of death toll."[19]

The earthquake hit on 27 March 1964. On 29 March, *The Washington Post* reported that "Washington" was directing "massive aid to the Alaskan earthquake victims."[20] The earthquake came late in the afternoon, at 5:36 p.m. The next day, LBJ had "declared a national disaster and dispatched members of the Office of Emergency Planning (OEP) to Alaska to get relief efforts rolling."

As historian Kevan Kosar wrote, "Johnson might have stopped here at the point of providing disaster relief. With civil rights issues brewing and a war in Vietnam going less than well, and a campaign to run against Barry Goldwater, the president was plenty busy. Instead, Johnson put his mind to formulating a plan to produce legislation that would provide rational plans for reconstructing the damaged areas. On April 2, he established through executive order the Federal Reconstruction and Development Planning Commission for Alaska (FRDPCA). It was an ingenious entity," consisting of members of various agencies, and the very effective senator from New Mexico, Clinton P. Anderson, who was adept at guiding legislation through the Senate. "FRDCPA took what it learned on the ground in Alaska (it held numerous forums with both local officials and the public) and drew up sensible legislation to enact policy that would promote the long-term recovery of Alaska. On May 27, just two months after the earthquake, LBJ submitted reconstruction legislation to Congress. By mid-August, Congress had enacted the bill into law and Alaska was on the road to full recovery. In October of 1964," LBJ abolished the Federal Reconstruction and Development Planning Commission for Alaska.[21] In its brief existence of fewer than seven months, his FRDCPA had completely fulfilled its mission, and LBJ ensured that it would not linger as a useless agency, thus demonstrating that an old criticism of government administration need not be true: when an agency is created, it remains forever, even after it has completed its mission and has nothing to do.

NOTES

1. For an expanded discussion of the US Government's role in handling the aftermath of the San Francisco earthquake (as well as other natural disasters) see Max J. Skidmore, "Anti-Government is not the Solution to the Problem—Anti Government Is the Problem," *Risk, Hazards, & Crisis in Public Policy*, 3:4 (December 2012); available at http://onlinelibrary.wiley.com/doi/10.1002/rhc3.15/epdf. Some of the material in this section is taken from this article.

2. USGS, "The Great 1906 San Francisco Earthquake," 2006; http://earthquake.usgs.gov/regional/nca/1906/18april/index.php; retrieved 15 June 2015.

3. U. S. Census Bureau, "100th Anniversary: San Francisco Earthquake—April 18." CB06-FFSE.02-2, (12 April 2006 reissued); http://www.census.gov/press-release/www/releases/archive; retrieved 23 April 2012; I also cited these figures in my article, "Anti-Government is Not the Solution to the Problem—Anti-Government Is the Problem: The Role of Ideology in Presidential Response to Natural Disasters From San Francisco to Katrina", *Risk Hazards & Crisis in Public Policy*, 3:4 (December 2012). Note, though, that on 15 June 2015, this Census Bureau press release could no longer be retrieved. Blanche Evans, however, also cited the same figures from the Census Bureau release, which she cited, and they remain available in her "1906 San Francisco Earthquake Housing is Valuable Piece of History," *Realty Times* (17 April 20006) http://realtytimes.com/todaysheadlines1/item/8698-20060418_quakehistory; retrieved 15 June 2015.

4. Victor H. Metcalf, Telegram to President Theodore Roosevelt (26 April 1906), San Francisco Museum, http://www.sfmuseum.org/1906/metcalf.html; retrieved 15 June 2015.

5. William Howard Taft, "Telegram to Funston," (18 April 1906), San Francisco Museum, http://www.sfmuseum.org/1906.2apres.html; retrieved 15 June 2015.

6. Bell, Chief of Staff, Telegram to Commanding General, Department of Columbia, Vancouver Barracks, Washington. (19 April 1906), San Francisco Museum. http://www.sfmuseum.org/photos2telegram2.gif; retrieved 15 June 2015.

7. Acting Secretary of War, Telegram to Commanding General, San Francisco. (26 April 1906). San Francisco Museum. http://www.sfmuseum.org/photos2telegram3.gif; retrieved 15 June 2015.

8. "History of the Medical Department (Excerpted), "Relief Work in San Francisco, California," and "Special Orders No. 37." (20 April 1906), San Francisco Museum. http://www.sfmuseum.org/1906/medical.html; retrieved 15 June 2015.

9. "Great Work By Signal Corps: Lines are run over Ruined Walls and Through Smoking Streets During Fire," *San Francisco Chronicle* (3 May 1906) San Francisco Museum. http://www.sfmuseum.net/conflag/signalcorps.html; retrieved 15 June 2015.

10. Brig. Gen. Frederick Funston, "How the Army Worked to Save San Francisco." *Cosmopolitan Magazine* XLI:3 (July 1906), San Francisco Museum. http://www.sfmuseum.org/1906/cosmo.html; retrieved 15 June 2015.

11. D. W. Coffman, D. W., "U.S.S. Boston," Report to Commander-in-Chief Pacific Squadron, (10 May 1906), San Francisco Museum. http://www.sfmuseum.org/1906/boston.html; retrieved 15 June 2015.

12. Carl Nolte, "The Great Quake: 1906–2006/ Rising from the Ashes." *San Francisco Chronicle* (18 April 2006); http://www.sfgate.com/news/article/The-Great-Quake-1906-2006-Rising-from-the-ashes-2537103.php ; retrieved 16 June 2015.

13. KateStohr, "San Fran's Lessons for New Orleans: How does a broken city pick up the pieces after a catastrophe? Here's what the Crescent City can take from the Great Earthquake of 1906." *Business Week* (12 September 2005).

14. Brian Williams, "LBJ's Political Hurricane," *The New York Times* (op ed) (24 September 2005), p. A.

15. "Transcript of Audio of President Johnson in New Orleans Following Landfall of Hurricane Betsy, September 10, 1965," LBJ Library http://www.lbjlib.utexas.edu/johnson/AV.hom/Hurricane/audio_transcript.shtm; retrieved 16 July 2015.

16. Williams, "L.B.J.'s Political Hurricane."

17. David Remnick, "Letter from Louisiana: High Water: How Presidents and Citizens React to Disaster." *The New Yorker* (3 October 2005).

18. James Lee Burke, *The Tin Roof Blowdown*. New York: Simon and Schuster, 2007, p. 98.

19. "Alaska: Prince William Sound, Alaska, Earthquake of March 27, 1964," no date. Vibration Data; http://www.vibrationdata.com/earthquakes/alaska.htm; retrieved 17 June 2015.

20. Charles Rabb, "Washington Directs Massive Aid to Alaska Earthquake Victims." *Washington Post* (29 March 1964), p. A6.

21. Kevin Kosar, 2005. "Rebuilding Hurricane-Devastated Areas—Why Not Follow LBJ's Lead?" *History News Network* (3 October 2005); http://hnn.us/articles/16383.html; retrieved 17 June 2015.

CHAPTER 5

President R. Gerald Ford

Abstract President Ford, when faced with the emergence of a virus that appeared to be related to the one that caused the horrendous pandemic of 1918, moved vigorously to prepare for the possibility of another such onslaught. There was widespread agreement that the possibility of another such pandemic existed, and that prudence demanded quick action. Securing quick approval from a Democratic Congress, the Republican president launched the National Influenza Immunization Program to vaccinate virtually the entire population.

Keywords Swine flu • President Ford • Playing politics with Pandemics • NIIP • Unfair condemnation • Conventional wisdom • Vaccines

VIGOROUS ACTION TO DEFEND AGAINST A THREATENED PANDEMIC

On 24 March 1976, President Gerald Ford—the only person ever to have held the office who had not been elected either president or vice-president—appeared before television cameras in a nationwide broadcast to announce to the country his decision to undertake the National Influenza Immunization Program (NIIP). He called for Congress to approve the

© The Author(s) 2016
M.J. Skidmore, *Presidents, Pandemics, and Politics*, The Evolving American Presidency, DOI 10.1057/978-1-137-59959-9_5

plan to vaccinate "every man, woman, and child" in the USA. The president's announcement was in response to the discovery on 27 January that a new strain of swine influenza virus had infected recruits at Fort Dix, New Jersey. There had been one death. On 4 February, one of the recruits, Private David Lewis, collapsed and died "after leaving his sick bed and making a forced, five-mile, night march."[1] Despite being controlled by Democrats, Congress acted quickly on the Republican president's request. President Ford signed the implementing legislation on 15 April.

FAIR GAME: THE POLITICS OF PILING ON

A little less than nine months later, on 16 December, the official in charge of NIIP, Assistant Secretary of Health, Education, and Welfare Theodore Cooper, M.D., announced the program's suspension. Some five weeks after that, Harry Schwartz, a member of the Editorial Board, published an op-ed piece in *The New York Times* bearing the title, "Swine Flu Fiasco."[2] Schwartz began, "The sorry debacle of the swine flu vaccine program provides a fitting end point to the misunderstandings and misconceptions that have marked Government approaches to health care during the last eight years, when Washington power has been shared between a Republican White House and a Democratic Congress." Schwartz asserted that "on the flimsiest of evidence, President Ford and the Congress were panicked into believing that the country stood at the threshold of a killer flu epidemic, one that might clam millions of lives as did the much-cited influenza pandemic of 1918–1919." Swartz gave no description of that "flimsy evidence," but simply pointed out that "today, there is no sign whatsoever of anything approaching a swine flu epidemic." Instead, he said, there is growing concern that the millions of dollars spent and expenditure of "all Washington's energies may have resulted in the death of some persons and sickened many more." He charged that the White House had a "scarcity" of officials with enough medical knowledge to "be able to put biological reality before political expediency." This, despite his conclusion that Ford and Congress had been "panicked into believing" that a lethal epidemic was coming. Either it was political expedience or a "panicked belief" that was mistaken; it could hardly have been both. Swartz condemns the government's health bureaucracy for self-interest, charging that it "saw in the swine flu threat the ideal chance to impress the nation with the capabilities of saving money and lives by preventing disease." So? Is that a bad thing? There were legitimate criticisms to hurl at Ford's plan, but such logical twists as Swartz employs as he seems to throw into the mix anything he can think of, regardless of consistency or evidence, were pure polemic, and should never have been taken seriously. Nevertheless, the sober researchers Neustadt and Fineberg, with their flippant approach, did so, and quoted the Swartz op-ed as if he could add weight to their conclusions.[3]

Jimmy Carter had succeeded Ford as president in January 1977. Joseph Califano, Carter's new secretary of health, education, and welfare, quickly fired Cooper (this is hardly unusual—incoming presidents more often than not replace sub-cabinet officers—but in this instance Califano was explicitly making a point), and also relieved David Sencer, M.D., director of the Centers for Disease Control.[4] Califano, too, spoke of NIIP as a "fiasco." He commissioned a formal report of the "fiasco" by two Harvard faculty members: political scientist and presidential scholar Richard Neustadt, and physician Harvey Fineberg—described by Carnegie Corporation President David Hamburg as "a leader in the new field of medical decision analysis."[5]

Califano published the report as an official document.[6] Neustadt and Fineberg later revised it, and published the later version as a book in 1983.[7] In what would seem to be an odd choice for two scholars to cite as a reliable source on a technical matter, the authors quoted an unnamed producer of Walter Cronkite's CBS show as saying that "it was a rotten program, rotten to the core. We thought it was politically inspired ... it certainly was awful in technical terms ... unwarranted ... unnecessary."[8]

Few if any analysts would attribute Ford's loss in 1976 to his swine flu program—the Nixon pardon was probably the most influential single issue, buttressed by the apparently fatigued president's stumbling performance when discussing Soviet domination of Eastern Europe in his debate with Carter—but NIIP likely contributed to Ford's defeat, and certainly did nothing to enhance his chances for victory. Public perception of the immunization plan had come to be overwhelmingly negative. The general assumption apparently was that if policymakers had anything to learn from the swine flu experience, it was how not to go about protecting the health of the public.

That assumption, in fact, seems to have become the conventional wisdom and to have persisted to this day, at least outside the circle of health-care professionals. Three years after NIIP ended, the CBS television news show "60 Minutes," although conceding in the opening segment that in 1976 "the threat posed by the swine flu virus seemed very real indeed," devoted its broadcast to some citizens who alleged harm from the vaccinations.[9]

After nearly three decades, *The Washington Post* in 2002 called NIIP "One of the biggest public health debacles in memory."[10] Even some health professionals went on record to share the jaundiced view. For example,

Kathleen Gensheimer, MD, MPH, of the Maine Department of Health and Human Services, in a generally thoughtful essay on pandemic planning, included a paragraph gratuitously headed, "Don't Repeat Swine Flu:"[11]

> The response to disease crises from yesterday should assist us in planning for the crises of tomorrow. We need to take seriously lessons learned from recent events such as SARS and smallpox vaccine initiatives and to incorporate those lessons in our pandemic planning efforts. We need to be proactive in our planning, not reactive; establish priorities for scarce resources; and invest in a wide range of activities that will enhance our collective response. We can't just "turn on the faucet" when the next crisis hits, but utilize limited resources strategically, allowing an effective collective response.

These are certainly sound observations. Regardless of the paragraph's heading, however, they have little or nothing to do with NIIP, other than to present it as worthless on all counts. The assumption is clearly that we can learn from SARS and smallpox vaccination initiatives, but from NIIP we learn nothing except that we should not repeat it.

Even scholars writing about the Ford administration often ignore NIIP entirely, or give it short shrift. Consider Douglas Brinkley's *Gerald R. Ford*, for example, a part of the Times Books series "The American Presidents."[12] This series offers books that are reasonably brief, but generally good, treatments of the various presidents. Brinkley's *Gerald Ford* is no exception, but with regard to the swine flu program, his book more than falls short. He devotes a mere two sentences—a piece of a paragraph—to the subject. They imply that there had been no real reason for NIIP. Moreover, "the vaccine caused temporary paralysis in some recipients," he wrote, "and even a few deaths."[13]

To be sure, there were some cases of Guillain-Barré syndrome that followed vaccination, and there was an elevated risk for those who had had the vaccine. The causes of this very rare affliction, though, are still not known. There has been no evidence that the vaccine was faulty, or that it "caused" the condition. Unquestionably, Brinkley is correct that the reaction to NIIP was disastrous for Ford's reputation, becoming, as he put it, a joke. To point that out, however, is not to demonstrate that matters were so simple as the critics asserted, or that Ford and his administration—considering the circumstances—had acted irrationally.

Brinkley is an excellent historian, with many superb books to his credit. He cites his source for his comments on Ford and the swine flu program as being a personal conversation with Richard Norton Smith. Smith is a well-known and respected biographer, historian, and sometime presidential library director. He has been director of the library of every Republican president from Hoover through Reagan, with the exception of Nixon's and including Ford's. The lesson from this is that even highly competent historians and other analysts can be led astray when an erroneous view becomes the conventional wisdom. When "everyone knows" something, it is too easy to assume that there is no need to investigate. This can create long traditions of faulty scholarship, as I make clear in my study of Gilded Age presidents.[14]

The more balanced perspective that seems so lacking requires a look beyond the headlines and the passions of the day, political and otherwise, and beyond received conventional wisdom. Such a look reveals that NIIP in some ways actually was successful, and that some of its lessons may be positive.

NOTES

1. Richard E. Neustadt and Harvey Fineberg, M.D., *The Swine Flu Affair*, Washington: U.S. Government Printing Office, 1978, p. 165.
2. Harry Schwartz, "Swine Flu Fiasco," *New York Times* (21 December, 1976), p. 33.
3. Neustadt and Finegold, pp. 97–98.
4. Arthur Silverstein, *Pure Politics an Impure Science*. Baltimore: Johns Hopkins University Press, 1981, p. 129.
5. David Hamberg in Neustadt and Fineberg, p. xi.
6. Neustadt and Fineberg, *The Swine Flu Affair*, 1978.
7. Richard Neustadt and Harvey Fineberg, M.D., Neustadt, *The Epidemic that Never Was: Policy-Making and the Swine Flu Affair* (a revised version of *The Swine Flu Affair*, 1978), New York: Vintage Books, 1983.
8. *Ibid.* p. 48.
9. *60 Minutes*, "Swine Flu," (4 November, 1979); available at http://www.whale.to/vaccines/swine.html, retrieved 7 June 2015.
10. David Brown, 2002. "A Shot in the Dark: Swine Flu's Vaccine Lessons," *Washington Post* (27 May 2002), p. A 9.
11. Kathleen Gensheimer, Kathleen, M.D., M.P.H., "Considerations for Pandemic Influenza Planning: A State Perspective," in *The Threat of Pandemic Influenza: Are We Ready? Workshop Summary*, ed. Stacey Knobler, et al., Washington: Institute of Medicine, National Academies Press, 2005, pp. 168–172; quoted paragraph on p. 171.
12. Douglas Brinkley, *Gerald Ford*, New York: Times Books/Henry Holt & Co., 2007.
13. *Ibid.*, p. 141.
14. See Max J. Skidmore, *Maligned Presidents: The Late 19th Century*, New York: Palgrave Macmillan, 2014.

CHAPTER 6

President Ford's National Influenza Immunization Program: A Special Case

Abstract Despite many obstacles, Ford's NIIP resulted in huge numbers of vaccinations. The pandemic, however, did not develop, and other considerations, some of them political, brought Ford's program into disrepute. It would be an exaggeration to say that it caused Ford's defeat in the election of 1976, but certainly it contributed.

The outcome led to the development of a popular view that accepted Ford's NIIP as a fiasco, perhaps even one that was purely motivated by politics. This chapter suggests that the time has come for a more nuanced interpretation; that Ford's program was well-intentioned, that the view that it was a failure is misguided, and that it offers subsequent health planners positive, as well as negative, examples for guidance.

Keywords HEW • President Ford • NIIP • Swine flu • CDC • Pandemics • Marketplace solutions • Vaccination • Legal issues ill-founded criticism

The Background: Widespread Agreement

Although the conventional wisdom would overwhelmingly appear to class NIIP as an inappropriate reaction to an impending threat, adverse media coverage has conditioned much of that view. Certainly the case is far from clear-cut. The discovery of a new swine flu virus at Fort Dix alarmed public health officials. They were well aware of the ravages of the 1918 flu, and

© The Author(s) 2016
M.J. Skidmore, *Presidents, Pandemics, and Politics*, The Evolving American Presidency, DOI 10.1057/978-1-137-59959-9_6

this virus appeared to be closely related to that of the pandemic of that time, if not in fact identical. The officials were concerned about a repetition of the tragedy, or the threat of perhaps an even more virulent pandemic.

President Ford had appointed F. David Mathews as secretary of health, education, and welfare in 1975. He took office on 8 August when he was still in his thirties, and by the time of the Fort Dix discovery, there had been little time for him to become known in Washington. Moreover, there may have been a tendency to dismiss him because of his relative youth and presumed inexperience. Nevertheless, he was a reasonably seasoned executive. The authors of the official study of NIIP say in their report that Mathews was "a gracious man, and graceful," but one who had come only recently to the department, and who "remained but a name" to most at HEW. As enormous as HEW's staff was, one can only wonder how they concluded that Mathews was less known to those who worked there than any other secretary had been. They continued that by Mathews's own account to them, he "had brought with him a deep feeling for preventive medicine," and that he thought that he and HEW's personnel "were philosophically in tune. From what they tell us," though, their report sniffed (with no mention of how many of HEW's personnel they had met—let alone interviewed), "most of them would find the thought surprising."[1]

Upon receiving his Ph.D. from Columbia University in 1965, Mathews accepted appointment as assistant professor of history at the University of Alabama. Within four years, he had become president of the university, having already served first as interim dean of men (which brought him to the attention of the university's central administration) and then as a vice-president. Despite his relative youth, Mathews had been a university president for some six years by the time he joined Ford's cabinet.

As the Fort Dix episode was unfolding, a highly relevant book was newly released, *Epidemic and Peace, 1918*, by Alfred W. Crosby.[2] According to Neustadt and Fineberg, Mathews was informed of the coincidental new book, and he "promptly ordered copies and sent them to associates in HEW, the Budget and the White House. He also gave one to Ford."[3] Although Mathews was no health professional, as Davis put it, he "was vividly aware of the carnage wrought by the 1918 pandemic."[4] He was therefore quite prepared to act.

Shortly after discovery of the new virus, both military and civilian health officials moved quickly to gather as much information as possible. After having positively identified the virus, CDC informed state health officials on 18 February of the presence of the new pathogen,[5] and subsequently released the information to the public. On 10 March, the Public Health Service's Advisory Committee on Immunization Practices (ACIP) concluded that a pandemic was possible, and that there needed to be an immunization program. "One ACIP member summarized the consensus by stating 'If we believe in prevention, we have no alternative but to offer and urge the immunization of the population.' One ACIP member expressed the view that the vaccine should be stockpiled, not given."[6] CDC Director David Sencer sent his "action memo" to Mathews on 13 March. The four options he outlined were: (1) "business as usual," i.e. relying on the marketplace; (2) "that the federal government embark on a major program to immunize a highly susceptible population," noting that additional expenditures were to be preferred over "unnecessary death and illness;" (3) a minimal program, securing and providing vaccine to "traditional federal beneficiaries," such as military personnel, Native Americans, and those on Medicare; and (4) "an exclusively federal response without involvement of the states."[7] Sencer strongly recommended the second option.

At a meeting with Secretary Mathews on 15 March, Sencer personally urged that there be mass immunization. That same day, Mathews wrote to the Director of the Office of Management and Budget (OMB), James Lynn, alerting OMB of the possibility of a major outbreak of disease, and warning that there might need to be a supplemental appropriation. President Ford then on 22 March met with Mathews and Assistant Secretary Theodore Cooper, M.D., from HEW; also at the meeting were officials from OMB and the White House staff. Before deciding upon the huge program, the president sought counsel from leading experts. A meeting took place two days later; among those present were polio vaccine pioneers Jonas Salk and Alfred Sabin.

This meeting would appear to be highly relevant to evaluations after the fact regarding NIIP—especially evaluations of Ford's decision—but it seems for the most part to have been ignored in the torrent of blame casting that took place, and has continued to influence comments on the program. "Sencer opened the meeting by reviewing the facts of the potential swine flu epidemic, as he saw them. Ford then asked Salk and Sabin for their opinion. Both were enthusiastically in favor." Ford called for a show of hands, asking all who "wanted the nation to proceed with a swine flu immunization effort to raise their hands. All did." The president did not let it rest. He told the group that he would dismiss the meeting, and invited anyone who might have reservations to meet with him privately in his office. "'Just get up, come over, knock, and walk in,' Ford told them. No one did."[8]

It bears repeating that this meeting took place, that none of the experts there expressed reservations, and that most subsequent assessments of the program ignored or dismissed it. Perhaps it was inconsistent with the mindset of the critics.

THE LAUNCHING OF FORD'S NIIP

That afternoon, 24 March, President Ford announced the program. Secretary Mathews and Assistant Secretary Cooper conducted a press conference, along with Sencer, Salk, and Sabin.[9] The questions ranged widely, from egg allergies (the virus for the vaccine would be grown in eggs) to cost. Regarding outreach, Cooper said:

> Yes. As part of our proposed activity, there are three main parts. One is the production and certification of high quality vaccine. We have been assured by the experts it is efficacious.
> Secondly is the organization of the system so that the capability of delivering it is present in any setting, including the financial barrier system that you just described, and thirdly is having the capability there without the public awareness and willingness to participate, would not be as successful campaign and, as was pointed out to the President, I believe by Dr. Sabin earlier, the previous campaigns that did not include an important awareness activity of this type were only 50 or 60 percent effective [sic]. So, the program that is proposed has all three elements.

Sencer noted that the swine flu vaccine would not displace production of vaccine for the Victoria strain that was currently circulating. The Victoria vaccine had already been produced, he said. Cooper said that the government would be paying for the vaccine, but not for the full cost of program administration. He said that physicians and public health officials were offering full cooperation, and that costs would vary. Those who chose to receive immunization from their private physicians would bear the cost of administration, while "others who go to public facilities may not have to pay, depending on what the arrangement is in a selected area." In any case, he said the program would not be completely federalized, and that the federal government would not be bearing the total cost.

On 31 March, Ford sent a memorandum to the heads of all departments and agencies. In the final paragraph he said, "Because the health of our nation is at stake, I intend to give this matter my direct and continuous attention, and I am asking each of you to make a similar commitment within your own organization."[10] Presidential involvement meant that

White House staff would be monitoring the program, and that duty fell to James Cavanaugh of the Domestic Council and his assistant, Spencer Johnson.[11] On 6 April, the president followed up with a memorandum to Secretary Mathews, directing Mathews and HEW to "assume the responsibility for this effort." Ford said that he intended to give the program his "direct and continuous attention," and that he expected to be kept informed regularly. To that end, he would require "a bi-weekly report from you indicating our progress toward the essential program goals and timetable targets." He added that this would be "the single most important public health undertaking by the Federal Government, and we must assure completion of the task in a proper and timely manner."[12]

OBSTACLES EMERGE

Despite the strong message from the White House, there were complications within HEW. Mathews wanted to be involved, but Cooper saw NIIP as his program. On 25 March, Mathews had asked Cooper to chair a department-wide committee that would meet daily to coordinate NIIP. Cooper saw it as a waste of time. He was "an activist, who liked to travel light and quickly; he wanted no ponderous committee to get in his way," so the committee began to meet less frequently. Thus, Mathews was never as involved as he had hoped to be. Later, it would become clear that circumventing the departmental committee had been a grave error. HEW's "Office of the General Counsel (OGC) worked for Mathews and not for Cooper. In the frenetic days of April 1976 swine flu was considered to be solely a health problem; in June and July serious legal difficulties would threaten to topple" the program, and "only then would the organizers wish that they had bought the lawyers in at an earlier stage."[13]

In addition, in "Atlanta, CDC's David Sencer felt that his was the lead agency in any immunization venture," while Cooper thought the responsibility should be his, since from his distant location, Sencer could not coordinate activities that included other necessary agencies, such as OMB, and NIAID (the National Institute of Allergies and Infectious Diseases). Nevertheless, requests for proposals to local agencies regarding vaccine distribution and consent procedures went out, and the "organization of the program proceeded fairly well."[14]

Trouble began to build throughout the spring as insurers decided they would not cover vaccine manufacturers to protect them against liability. The manufacturers, in turn, indicated that they would refuse to participate without protection from the government. Ultimately, on 12 August—

after considerable argument in Congress and elsewhere, after attempts from HEW to deal with the insurance industry, and even after pleas to various parties from the White House itself had failed—President Ford signed the Tort Claims act.[15] Silverstein pointed out that these obstacles were significant: "the two-month delay imposed by the insurance problem exacted a heavy toll on the swine flu program."[16] He wrote caustically that "it was obvious that the insurance industry had won its fight with the government. Despite all of the name-calling in Congress, in HEW, and even in the White House, the insurance companies had successfully resisted involvement in the swine flu immunization program. For the first time, they had forced the government of the United States to declare itself ready to insure one of its public health programs."[17] He said that if Ford had not personally become involved in announcing and supporting the program, the administration might have let it die, rather than putting government into the insurance business.

There had already been delays, even before the roadblocks that the insurance companies created. Cooper had announced on 2 June that one of the manufacturers had used the wrong virus in producing two million doses.[18] The vaccine they had produced was not dangerous, but was ineffective. Other delays occurred because of determining the proper dosage and the most effective method of vaccine administration for children.

Immunizations finally began on 1 October.[19] Silverstein noted the inadequate mobilization of private physicians, who were so important to the effort. In spite of all the problems, though, by December 16 some 45,650,199 doses of swine flu vaccine had been administered to the civilian population of the United States, as well as about 1 ½ million more given to the military and to dependents by the Department of Defense. This was estimated to have covered about 24 percent of the entire eligible population.[20] This was in spite of numerous obstacles placed in the program's way. Even some of the critics through the years who have scoffed at the program have been compelled to concede that this was a substantial accomplishment. What few, if any, have recognized—perhaps because it goes against the carefully manipulated "conventional wisdom"—is that this feat presents a clear demonstration that when the will exists, the Government of the USA can quickly gear for action, and can perform very effectively indeed.

Gina Kolata, a respected science journalist for *The New York Times*, conducted a study of the 1918 pandemic, and expanded her examination to the difficulties faced by Ford's National Influenza Immunization Program. As she put it, "the trouble began almost immediately." She wrote that "the very day President Ford made his announcement...critics who had kept mum until that crucial moment suddenly surfaced."[21] "Effect Measure," a website devoted to public health discussion, spoke of the media attention to some strong disagreements from a "few scientists, some within the government," and noted that the disagreements had been "hitherto unvoiced." Among the rearguard critics and the unfavorable press reports, Dr. Sabin raised his prominent voice, joining the critics. He had changed his mind, and came to believe that stockpiling the vaccine, not mass immunization, would have been the proper approach.

Under the circumstances, however, the logic undergirding the program was powerful. Kolata quoted a former Harvard professor of public health, Geoffrey Edsall, who had heard about the program of mass vaccination while in the presence of officials of the Bureau of Biologics of the Food and Drug Administration; he had then questioned the wisdom of acting on such slim information. The official replied, "Look, I know that the chance of a pandemic may be as little as 1 to 50 or even less, but if *you* were the President of the United States and were told that the country faced a 1 to 50 or maybe even a 1 to 100 chance of a national disaster—which on the basis of all available evidence could largely be averted by a vaccine program—what would you say?" Edsall said, "I got the point."[22] That simple comment may well have been the most cogent observation of the entire controversy.

The vaccine shortage was a strong blow. As odd as it might seem, though, the death knell for NIIP resulted from the extraordinary effectiveness of the monitoring system that the officials had implemented to check on the program. There previously had been concerns among the public. News reports stressed that some who had received the vaccine had died not long after. This of course was inevitable, and was to have been expected. Among the millions of recipients, some would have died in any case, regardless of whether they had received the vaccine. It was clearly established that the deaths were unrelated to the vaccine, but that failed to soften the impression that writers and newscasters were conveying. As August began, there were dramatic reports of sudden, mysterious, deaths in Philadelphia among those attending an American Legion convention. The ailment at first suggested swine flu, but was quickly determined to be a new form of pneumonia, bacterial in nature, that was unrelated to influenza.[23]

These cases added to the sense of urgency regarding a vaccination program, but their importance to the overall endeavor was as nothing compared to the discovery later, that among those who had been vaccinated were cases of Guillain-Barré syndrome (GBS). This is a rare "disorder in which the body's immune system attacks part of the peripheral nervous system." Most patients recover, but some suffer permanent weakness, and some cases do lead to death. The condition usually occurs "a few days or weeks after the patient has had symptoms of a respiratory or gastrointestinal viral infection. Occasionally, surgery or vaccinations will trigger the syndrome."[24]

The cases were sporadic, and remained rare. There was, and still is, no definitive evidence of causation. Nevertheless, there was clearly an increased risk of contracting GBS for those who had received the vaccination. As Silverstein put it, although the number of cases of GBS was not large, there was a statistically-significant increase in risk—GBS is always present in the population, and those receiving the vaccine had roughly a sevenfold increase in likelihood of contracting the syndrome. The overall numbers were tiny in relation to the huge population involved, but however low the increase in numbers was, that increase was definitely present. "What is especially ironic," Silverstein wrote, was "that the relationship would have been missed completely had the planners of the National Immunization Program not taken great care in setting up their surveillance system. The influenza vaccine conference of March 21, 1977, concluded that the 'risks of influenza vaccine are so low that, had there not been a sensitive special vaccine reaction surveillance system, and had not over 40 million doses of vaccine been given in a two-month period, the relationship between influenza vaccine and GBS would not have been detected.'"[25]

Sencer himself described the outcome. "Had H1N1 influenza been transmitted at that time," he wrote, "the small apparent risk of GBS from immunization would have been eclipsed by the obvious immediate benefit of vaccine-induced protection against swine flu." Since swine flu was not spreading, however, the vaccination of over 40 million persons led federal officials to decide that "the possibility of an association of GBS with the vaccine, however small, necessitated stopping immunization." The moratorium announced on 16 December 1976 "effectively ended NIIP."[26] The new Carter administration was only too happy to leave the program behind, casting a negative reflection on the defeated President Ford.

No Pandemic Plus Health Risk Must Mean Fiasco: A Confused Discourse

"From that point on, swine flu became synonymous with political fiasco," wrote Mike Davis, a historian described in his book's blurb as "America's most incendiary urban critic. "Carter's new HEW [Department of Health,

Education, and Welfare] secretary, Joseph Califano, asked two Harvard scholars, Richard Neustadt and Harvey Fineberg, to undertake a case-study of the Ford administration's response to the Fort Dix outbreak. Although Neustadt and Fineberg discovered a definite chain of error," Davis said, "they found it impossible to dismiss the CDC's original apprehensions as irrational or irresponsible. Indeed, Califano himself later conceded that he would have probably made the same decision as Mathews, his ill-fated predecessor." Davis pointed out that expert opinion leaned toward the notion that over-reaction was better than no reaction, that it would be better to have a "vaccine without an epidemic than an epidemic without a vaccine," but that there was little sympathy in Congress. He said the most vicious backlash came not from Ford's opposition Democrats, but from "the Reagan wing of the Republican Party." In 1978, Carter attempted to fund a permanent flu vaccination program, but Republican Senator Richard Schweiker of Pennsylvania scoffed at the idea. When Reagan took the presidency in 1981 following the 1980 elections, Schweiker became his new secretary of Health and Human Services (the department that replaced HEW when the Office of Education was stripped out and granted cabinet status as the Department of Education). Given Ronald Reagan's long-held antipathy toward most governmental programs, the prospects for any new health efforts were non-existent. "Privatization" and de-regulation were the preferred approaches. Sure enough, the new administration cut funding for immunization programs, and "influenza vaccine was handed back to a pharmaceutical industry that had less enthusiasm than ever for the product." Efforts to expand immunization programs were "stopped cold."[27]

It is correct that Neustadt and Fineberg could identify no villains. In their introduction to the published study, they professed to have been "cheered mightily," when Califano, after reading their draft, conceded that he had changed his mind about assessing blame. No longer thinking of NIIP as a "fiasco," they wrote, he "had now concluded he himself or anybody else might have made the same swine flu decision as the previous Administration had done in 1976...this was the initial, perhaps even the chief, of the lessons we sought to convey." They "felt sure," therefore, that they had succeeded in making the case that "the complexities and uncertainties of the swine flu case transcended personalities or parties."[28]

It is difficult to read Neustadt and Fineberg's professed intentions, and then to examine both the popular and professional reactions to NIIP without a sense of wonderment. As harsh as it sounds, this team of "one of the most distinguished scholars in the field of governmental organization and high-level decision-making," and "an outstanding physician and a leader in the new field of medical decision analysis," as David Hamburg, President of the Carnegie Corporation, put it in his Foreword to their book,[29] were either too incompetent as writers to get their meaning across, or else were so flippant as to border on the irresponsible.

Regardless of their intentions and their stated "confidence," NIIP not only retained its bad reputation, which has affected the reputations of its planners, but those who decry the efforts of those planners *frequently cite Neustadt and Fineberg as their source for their negative opinions!* This is easy to understand when reading the report. Califano's reaction notwithstanding, the breezy language that the authors employed often sent mixed messages, and worked to convey anything but complexity and blame avoidance.

Sencer, for example, was "an able, wily, autocrat."[30] "Sencer was not President. Yet as he did his work this may be a distinction without a difference. For he evidently thought it was his task to make his constitutional superiors do right no matter what they thought (and so he did). He also made them do it with but little time to think." Moreover, that "they were his constitutional superiors...gave him no pause. Cooper aside, they were laymen. Sencer evidently held the not uncommon premise that the boobs could not be trusted to decide right on their own." That, the authors thought, was what made Sencer "a salesman."[31] "What a basis," they wrote scornfully, for Sencer "to build public consciousness and to seek support for preventive medicine! What a basis on which to risk the high repute of an establishment like CDC!" Even worse, what a basis "on which to expose 40 million people to an unknown risk of side effects!"[32]

They concluded—contradicting their own statement that anyone might have made the same decisions considering the evidence then available—that "in the absence of *manifest* danger, all-out action was a mistake." It was reasonable to begin manufacture of a vaccine at the first indication of possible need, "but one cannot reasonably stick it into people without more concrete evidence than anybody had at any time in 1976."[33] Yet it was their intention "to point no fingers, and to present the complexities of the situation." Perhaps—no, certainly—part of their trouble was their language. They chose "the form, tone, style, sentence structure and even word choice of the report" to present a case, rather than to produce a scholarly study with sources identified, or, one suspects, even to retain accuracy. They did it "to keep a busy and beset man *reading*." In other words, they thought that to keep Califano's attention, they had to make their work interesting (perhaps they shared what they said was Sencer's attitude toward "boobs" in positions of authority). One suspects that this goal at times superseded, or at least overshadowed, the requirement or concern for objectivity.

When Arthur Silverstein—who subsequently wrote the most penetrating study of NIIP—read the Neustadt and Fineberg report, he was amazed. Silverstein was from the Johns Hopkins University Medical School—an ophthalmic immunologist. He was intimately familiar with NIIP, because he was on sabbatical during the swine flu episode, serving with Sen. Edward Kennedy's Senate subcommittee on health. He thus not only observed the developments first hand, but actually participated. By the time the report came out nearly two years had elapsed, and Silverstein had returned to Hopkins.

Silverstein was amazed, and it is equally amazing that some discussions of NIIP actually report that he condemned the program and its architects. Apparently, many of the critics got little further into Silverstein's book than its title, *Pure Politics and Impure Science*. It is easy to see why readers of Neustadt and Fineberg might misunderstand what they said their intentions were, but Silverstein writes clearly and thoughtfully, and critics misinterpreted his work as well.

An otherwise thoughtful article in *The Trentonian* was typical. It said that "among the critics are Arthur M. Silverstein, whose book, 'Pure Politics and Impure Science,'" suggests President Gerald Ford's desire to win the office on his own, as well as the influence of America's big drug manufacturers, figured into the decision to immunize all 220 million Americans."[34]

Silverstein said no such thing, and this distorted his conclusions to the point of misrepresentation. Despite the article's assertions, Silverstein made it plain that when he spoke of "politics" as having "entered into the consideration at different stages," he implied nothing "dirty or underhanded." Rather, his stay in the Senate taught him to consider "politics" as in no way pejorative. Instead, political actions came to represent to him actions that responded to the will of the people, and "politics" came to mean "the art of the possible." Very little legislation, he discovered, resulted without "some degree of concessions, trade-offs, and compromise."[35] Nor, he might have added, in a democracy could it be otherwise.

He wrote that upon reading the report by Neustadt and Fineberg, he initially found himself muttering "That's not what really happened," and "My God! They left out the fascinating part about..." He had felt that somehow "Neustadt and Fineberg had gotten it all wrong." On reflection, though, he concluded that "the swine flu report was not erroneous in describing *what* had happened, but... [that] it was far off the mark in explaining *why* certain things happened."[36] This greatly concerned him, because "a misperception of what had happened in 1976 could cripple government efforts to cope with the next massive influenza pandemic, which," he said, "will surely come sometime in the future."[37]

During that fateful winter, swine flu did not recur in the USA or elsewhere. Had it done so, as Sencer (quoted above) said, the swine flu vaccination program would immediately have been reinstituted. A few hundred cases of GBS, even with dozens of deaths, "would have been considered a small price to pay to prevent thousands or tens of thousands of deaths from virulent influenza."[38]

As it was, on 27 January 1977, barely a week after Califano took office as the head of HEW, an outbreak of A/Victoria flu flared up in a nursing home in Miami. He concluded that the risk from widespread flu would far overshadow any risk from GBS, even though "the A/Victoria vaccine was available only in the bivalent formulation: in combination with the swine flu vaccine." After consulting with numerous authorities he relied on the advice of experts and "decided to release the bivalent vaccine;" that is, he decided that there would be additional use of the swine flu vaccine, since it would necessarily accompany the A/Victoria vaccine that the new outbreak required. He learned, he said, how enormous is the "difficulty that a lay official has in fulfilling his responsibility to make sound, balanced judgments about complex scientifically-based public health issues."[39]

Silverstein documented the escalation in language that led up to the decision to implement NIIP. On 10 March, the scientists in Atlanta had spoken of "some possibility of a pandemic." Three days later, Sencer's action memorandum used the words "strong possibility." Two days after that, Mathews had written to OMB Director Lyons that "there is evidence there will be a major flu epidemic." In noting the jump within five days from "some possibility" to "will be," Silverstein was not condemning the officials. He said that it "undoubtedly reflected the growing sense of urgency," and also speculated that it might also have reflected "one of the important realities of any large organization," especially government. The higher one proceeds up the hierarchy, the more generalists take over from specialists. Therefore, "government officials usually know that the higher the level at which a decision is sought, the simpler and starker and more compelling must be the presentation. At the lower levels of the bureaucracy, he said, "understanding of the scientific realities indicated that it could *and should* be done; at the higher levels, an understanding of the political realities indicated that it *must* be done."[40] There is nothing sinister about this, nor does it indicate that a given decision—or the decision to go ahead with NIIP—

was in any way based upon President Ford's desire to get re-elected. That did not, however, prevent editorialists, hostile political figures, or opponents of NIIP from assuming that Ford's re-election was the major factor in his decision to embark upon the program of mass immunization.

Silverstein considered the "seven principal features" that the Neustadt and Fineberg report concluded "characterized the program, and contributed to its ultimate failure." (1) The scientists had too much confidence in their theories, and had too little evidence upon which to base their recommendations. (2) Pre-existing "personal agendas" were involved, and drove decisions. Specifically, the authors "appear almost unwilling to concede any honorable basis for action to certain of the participants, most notably CDC's Sencer." (3) The government health professionals had an "almost unhealthy zeal...to make their lay superiors 'do the right thing.' Neustadt and Fineberg appear to agree that Sencer, by the words he chose in drafting his action memorandum, 'held a gun to the head of the President' and forced Ford to accede to the recommendation for a National Immunization Program." (4) Sencer and his advisers "decided too much too early," and Cooper acquiesced. (5) The planners ignored many uncertainties, and made no provision to reconsider the direction of, or even the need for, the program. (6) There was insufficient questioning of the scientific logic of the program, or of the likelihood of its success. (7) All officials involved, especially from CDC, demonstrated "profound insensitivity" to the news media, and failed to consider the implications of program failure for other agencies or programs. Nevertheless, "the authors rejected the notion that politics, partisan or otherwise, had any effect on the sequence of events."[41] Their conclusion that politics was not involved in the decision to pursue NIIP, though, did not prevent Neustadt and Fineberg from employing language that overwhelmed their sound conclusion, language that led many readers to conclude that they were implying otherwise.

Turning from Talking Points to Analysis: NIIP as a Learning Experience

As a rejoinder to Neustadt and Fineberg, Silverstein produced his own list of conclusions. Most of these were different from the report's, but some reflected agreement with those of Neustadt and Fineberg. (1) The decision to mount NIIP was correct. "All of the participants, including Sencer, Cooper, Mathews, Ford, and the scientific advisers acted in what they felt were the best interests of the American people." (2) The initial decision to vaccinate, rather than stockpile the vaccine, was also correct, considering the rapid spread of influenza pandemics and the "previous safety record of influenza vaccines." On the other hand, it would have been wise to have reconsidered the decision in August, when the pandemic failed to develop, when productions fell behind schedule, and when "public acceptance of the program had started to wane." (3) The administration of NIIP was conscientious, if somewhat inept. (4) "There were no real 'culprits' in 1976." All involved attempted conscientiously to do the best, but "all were caught up in a vortex of unpredictable events."[42]

The reason that Silverstein decided to write his own book was to offer "lessons to be learned." Without them, misunderstanding of what happened with regard to NIIP could bring "future timidity" that might someday lead to "millions of cases of illness and perhaps tens of thousands of deaths."[43] His thoughtful book should have accomplished its purpose, but, sadly, through no fault of his, it did not.

The public—insofar as it remembers NIIP at all—almost assuredly has a distorted view. Similar distortions may sometimes exist even among health professionals also, but they are likely to see the wisdom of his recommendations. Silverstein suggested that it would probably be wise to separate the decision to produce vaccine from the decision to immunize, and that the announcement of any program should probably come at the lowest level possible. "Perhaps Gerald Ford was right in 1976 in thinking that only the prestige of the presidency could assure successful implementation of the swine flu immunization program," he said, but "in doing so, he severely limited the options of those below him in HEW to reconsider..." Silverstein called also for automatic and periodic reevaluation of premises and reconsideration of decisions, as well as consistent reexamination of timetables and predictions. Those who manage a program must be skilled at management, not merely the skilled professionals who recommend it. He also pointed out the essential nature of public relations, and the need to deal with liability issues in advance.[44]

Any governmental decision, especially one so momentous, will inevitably reflect political elements. President Ford was genial and well-liked in Washington, and he was certainly no extremist, but he was strongly partisan. As minority leader of the House of Representatives, for example, he had permitted himself to be drawn into the abortive and unwise effort to impeach Justice William O. Douglas. His decision to pardon Richard Nixon may appear in retrospect to have been prudent, but his partisan record made some contemporary observers conclude otherwise, and it inflamed political passions. Moreover, Ford had a slow manner of speaking that inspired caricature, and several times he was caught on camera stumbling. Thus, this graceful, athletic man who impressed those who worked closely with him as having a keen mind and a thorough grasp of the issues became the subject of comics who portrayed him not only as clumsy, but also as not very bright. Chevy Chase devoted his early career to such a characterization.

In fact, some aspects of Ford's regime actually appear worse in retrospect: it would have been impossible to have foreseen the consequences at the time, of course, but by surrounding himself with figures such as Donald Rumsfeld and Richard Cheney, and by resuscitating the career of George H. W. Bush, he laid the groundwork for what was to become the Bush dynasty that culminated in the presidency of the younger Bush.

That presidency, far more extreme than Ford's despite Ford's own strong (but principled) conservatism, brought direct attacks on Social Security, elevated the religious right to a formidable influence on domestic and foreign policy, and created an aggressive foreign policy heavily dominated by those calling themselves Straussians. Straussians such as Paul Wolfowitz, William Kristol, and Richard Perle supported by Donald Rumsfeld and Dick Cheney long before 9/11 had been openly urging attacks upon Iraq even during the Clinton administration with their "Project for a New American Century, or PNAC."[45] This pressure came from outside Clinton's administration, and Clinton wisely disregarded it. When the younger Bush became president, he incorporated these figures and many others as integral parts of his administration, and unwisely took many of them into his inner circle, and their principles to heart.

Nevertheless, Ford's decision to approve NIIP should stand by itself. It appears clearly to have been based on concern for the public good, not to achieve political advantage.

The decision process may have been "messy"—as described by Neustadt and Fineberg, Silverstein, Kolata, and Crosby—but when Ford announced the program on television, "his view was that if everyone were to be asked to take the vaccine, the request should come from the President. It was in fact an act of courage on his part, as it was understood it was a no win situation politically," while Ford was involved with a primary struggle against Reagan. Moreover, a blogger at "Effect Measure"— calling itself a forum for progressive health discussion and argument, and a source of public health information—remarked in 2005, almost three decades later, that "it is not easy to imagine the current incumbent [George W. Bush] taking this route."[46]

ASSESSMENT OF NIIP

In his assessment of NIIP, Silverstein provides perspective by asking, reasonably, what the result would have been if the program had not existed, and if the pandemic had, indeed, developed. With "millions falling ill all around the country," and a rapidly-rising death toll, there would have been "appeals for a nonexistent swine flu vaccine and complaints about the inadequacies of the immunization program [that] would have reached a very shrill level indeed." He presented the spectacle of a Secretary Califano "commissioning an analogous study to find out what had gone wrong, resulting in the probable indictment of Sencer and Cooper for having decided too little too late!"[47] The phrase "damned if you do, and damned if you don't" comes to mind when reading standard assessments of Ford's NIIP. Silverstein at least helps to offset the conventional wisdom.

It is easy to identify flaws in the program—they are examined above and it is unnecessary to repeat them here—but it is simple-minded to conclude that they constituted its entirety. One may as easily view what NIIP did accomplish as a lesson teaching the potential of government action. It is necessary to act based on available information, not on information that unfolds over months or years to come. A lethal pandemic appeared to threaten. In the face of tremendous odds, a program emerged that provided protection to a record number of Americans, some 45 million, with unprecedented speed. Had the pandemic materialized, the number vaccinated would have been far greater. Moreover, the government's professionals designed a highly sophisticated and effective monitoring system that made it possible to have precise information regarding the program's effects. These were major accomplishments, for which the Ford administration deserves praise, not blame. Those who study the past to gain insights when preparing defenses against pandemics in the future should study Ford's NIIP for all the lessons it might teach, not merely to learn what to avoid.

NOTES

1. Richard E. Neustadt, and Harvey Fineberg, M.D., *The Epidemic that Never Was: Policy-Making and the Swine Flu Affair*, New York: Vintage Books, 1983, p. 32; Note: this new edition is not a revised version of the

official government report (*The Swine Flu Affair*, Washington: Government Printing Office, 1978). Rather, it is that report, plus additions: it reprints the report, includes a new Foreword by David Hamburg, President of the Carnegie Corporation; a new Introduction by the authors in addition to the original Introduction; and extensive appendices not in the original report.

2. Alfred W. Crosby, Jr., *Epidemic and Peace, 1918*, Westport, Connecticut: Greenwood Press, 1976.
3. Neustadt and Fineberg, p. 35.
4. Mike Davis, *The Monster at Our Door: The Global Threat of Avian Flu.* New York: Henry Holt, 2006, p. 41.
5. Neustadt and Fineberg, p. 166.
6. David J. Sencer, and J. Donald Millar, "Reflections on the 1976 Swine Flu Vaccination Program," *Emerging Infectious Diseases*, CDC (5 January 2006), p. 2; http://www.cdc.gov/ncidod/EID/vol12no1/05-1007.htm; retrieved 18 June 2015.
7. *Ibid.*
8. Gina Kolata, *Flu: The Story of the Great Influenza Pandemic of 1918 and the Search for the Virus that Caused it*, New York: Touchstone (Simon and Schuster) 2005, pp. 148–149.
9. Press Conference: Mathews, Salk, Sabin, Cooper, and Sencer, Transcript, Congressional Relations Office, Loen and Leppert Files, Box No. 24, Swine Flu folder 1, Gerald R. Ford Presidential Library (24 March 1976).
10. Gerald Ford, Gerald, "Memorandum for the Heads of Departments and Agencies 31 March, 1976, "Congressional Relations Office Collection," Swine Flu Folder 1, Box 24, Loen and Leppert Files, Gerald R. Ford Presidential Library.
11. Arthur Silverstein, Arthur, *Pure Politics an Impure Science*. Baltimore: Johns Hopkins University Press, 1981, p. 76.
12. Gerald Ford, Gerald, "Memorandum for the Secretary of Health, Education, and Welfare [Mathews]," 6 April 1976. "Domestic Council Collection, James M. Cannon," Swine Flu, April 1–12 1976 folder, Box No. 34, Gerald R. Ford Presidential Library.
13. Silverstein, p. 76.
14. *Ibid.*, pp. 77 and 79.
15. Neustadt and Fineberg, p. 18.
16. Silverstein, p. 107.
17. *Ibid.*, p. 95.
18. Neustadt and Fineberg, p. 175.
19. Neustadt and Fineberg, p 187.

20. Silverstein, p. 115.
21. Gina Kolata, *Flu: The Story of the Great Influenza Pandemic of 1918 and the Search for the Virus that Caused it*, New York: Touchstone (Simon and Schuster), 2005, p. 159.
22. *Ibid.*, p. 154.
23. Neustadt and Fineberg, p. 85.
24. "NINDS Guillain-Barre Syndrome Information Page," National Institute of Neurological Disorders and Stroke (23 January 2008). http://www.ninds.nih.gov/disorders/gbs/gbs.htm?css+print; retrieved 20 June 2015.
25. Silverstein, pp. 121–122.
26. Sencer and Millar, p. 4.
27. Davis, pp. 43–44.
28. Neustadt and Fineberg, pp. xx.
29. David Hamburg, "Foreword," *Ibid.*, pp. x–xi.
30. Neustadt and Fineberg, p. 23.
31. *Ibid.*, p. 132.
32. *Ibid.*, p. 133.
33. *Ibid.*, p. 136.
34. Paul Mickle "1976: Fear of a Great Plague," *The Trentonian* (not dated, but published in the 1990s); http://www.capitalcentury.com/1976.html; retrieved 20 June 2015.
35. Silverstein, p. xii.
36. *Ibid.*, p. xiii.
37. *Ibid.*, p. xiv.
38. *Ibid.*, p. 120.
39. Neustadt and Fineberg, p. 4.
40. Silverstein, pp. 42–43.
41. *Ibid.*, pp. 130–131.
42. *Ibid.*, pp. 140–141.
43. *Ibid.*, p. 141.
44. *Ibid.*, p. 142.
45. For information on the PNAC, see http://www.informationclearing-house.info/article1665.htm; retrieved 22 June 2015.
46. "Specter of 1976," *Effect Measure* (27 October 2005), at http://effect-measure.blogspot.com/2005/10/specter-1976.html; retrieved 22 June 2015.
47. Silverstein, p. 133.

CHAPTER 7

Conclusions

Abstract It is clear that Washington has had a checkered past with regard to emergency management, whether from geological or biological causes. This is no less true of the country's recent history. FEMA, the Federal Emergency Management Agency, presents superb examples, both of inexcusably poor performance and of sterling response to great need. The agency demonstrates that the quality and character of political leaders make the difference between a failed agency and one that performs quickly and effectively. Almost identical lessons can be learned from the Veterans' Health Administration. At times, the agency has been among the government's most justifiably criticized; at other times, it has supplied world-class health care unexcelled in this country. The differences in performance reflect the political philosophies, and the skills, of the country's top governmental leaders. The lessons to be learned should be obvious, but apparently they are not obvious enough. They should be stressed continually.

The country is a long way from overcoming years of mismanagement and ideological excess. Ultimately, American security depends upon completely recreating our infrastructure—both physical and institutional, employing delicate monitoring systems, emphasizing broad public education (including health education), and ensuring universal health care.

© The Author(s) 2016   77
M.J. Skidmore, *Presidents, Pandemics, and Politics*, The Evolving
American Presidency, DOI 10.1057/978-1-137-59959-9_7

Keywords Public administration • Effective government • Failings of private sector • Quality of service • Mismanagement

EMERGENCY MANAGEMENT

It is clear that emergency management, whether in response to geological or biological needs, has had a checkered past. This is no less true of our recent history.

The country's governors had long been concerned about the chaotic nature of the US Government's great variety of emergency response programs. During the Carter administration, the National Governors' Association urged President Jimmy Carter to provide coordination to simplify the overly complex nature of federal disaster response. President Carter agreed, and in 1979 he issued an executive order creating the Federal Emergency Management Agency (FEMA).

Far from taking care of the situation, though, during the twelve years following Carter's departure from office—that is, under the administrations of Ronald Reagan and George H. W. Bush—FEMA became a dumping ground for unqualified political appointments. It rapidly became recognized for its incompetence and overly bureaucratic procedures. It had "10 times the proportion of political appointees of most other government agencies." Defense against nuclear attack became its primary responsibility, and the inevitable natural disasters showed FEMA at its worst. It became notorious for refusing to respond until it received a formal request from the governor of the state or states involved, with every section of a complex report filled out exactly as the procedure required, and then sent through the US mail to FEMA's offices.[1]

FEMA received the reforms it needed in 1993, when the new president, Bill Clinton, named James Lee Witt, to head the agency, granted it "Cabinet-level status, and gave it a highly visible role it had not previously had." It responded quickly and effectively "to crises such as the 1995 Oklahoma City bombing..."[2] Witt was a professional who oriented the agency toward realities. Natural disasters would happen, regardless. Nuclear attacks, on the other hand, especially since the Soviet Union had dissolved, were unlikely, so he directed the agency toward what it would certainly be called upon to do.

Elsewhere, I have cataloged the outcome.[3] "Virtually overnight, the agency...developed a new reputation for quickness and efficiency." Within five hours of the Oklahoma City bombing, "FEMA's advance team arrived, complete with damage assessors and embers of Witt's staff. Six hours later... Witt himself arrived," and within another six hours, FEMA search and rescue teams were aiding the city's fire department. Similarly, when floods devastated Iowa in 1993, the city water supply of Des Moines was collapsing. One telephone call to a local FEMA field office early in the morning brought a detailed plan by noon; emergency water purification machines were in place, and supplying the city's residents with water by that evening.[4]

Another salient example that is more directly relevant to the topic of pandemics is the Veterans' Health Administration (VHA) in the Department of Veterans' Affairs. Scandal and bureaucratic inefficiency were the major components of its reputation. Then, in 1994, as with FEMA, President Clinton made a dramatic shift to competence and efficiency. He appointed Kenneth W. Kizer, M.D., to head the agency. He also held the title of undersecretary for health for the Veterans' Administration. Kizer quickly re-organized the VHA, aided by strong support that came directly from the president. Almost immediately, it became by many accounts the country's most efficient health organization. Study after study praises its quality of care, so much so that Phillip Longman could quite legitimately title his book on the subject *Best Care Anywhere: Why VA Health Care is Better than Yours.*[5] Like James Lee Witt at FEMA, Kizer completely transformed the VHA in record time.

"How FEMA transformed itself from what many considered to be the worst federal agency (no small distinction) to among the best is the most dramatic success story of the federal government in recent years. Not only does it provide further evidence that the government can work, it offers a blueprint for what it takes: strong leadership, energetic oversight, and, most importantly, a total reevaluation of its mission."[6] Both the VHA and FEMA made dramatic turnarounds in what by Washington standards was overnight. Witt and Kizer, of course, were keys, but the changes they brought, as Franklin said of FEMA, are "to varying degrees within the capabilities of any government agency or department with strong leadership."[7]

Unfortunately, that can work both ways. Any agency's effectiveness can also be destroyed. The VHA, despite being starved for funds by the priorities of George W. Bush's administration and its obsession with tax cuts, has fared far better than FEMA (even though the VHA, because of its shriveled funding, has had its share of scandals). As soon as Bush followed Clinton into the White House, he replaced Witt at FEMA, and proceeded to pack the agency with political cronies, regardless of qualifications. The resulting incompetence was plain for the entire country to see when FEMA blundered into New Orleans following Katrina.

An editorial in *USA Today* asserted that FEMA's Katrina failures were not "a momentary burst of poor decisions. Over the past four years," the editorial said, Bush's administration had "replaced competent leaders with people long on political connections but short on disaster management expertise," while at the same time "the war on terrorism has drained the agency's resources and reduced its effectiveness."[8] The director of the King County, Washington, Office of Emergency Management said that the "advent of the Bush administration in January 2001 signaled the beginning of the end of FEMA." By removing the "disaster preparedness function" that had been its responsibility since the beginning, he said, the Bush administration dealt a "death blow to an agency that was already on life support."[9] An article in *The Washington Post* summed it up. After 9/11 "FEMA lost out in the massive bureaucratic shuffle." The agency not only lost its cabinet status but also its budget. After re-organization, the government spends some $20 billion annually against terrorist attacks that may occur, and only about $180 million against natural hazards that are inevitable.[10]

LESSONS TO BE LEARNED

There are definite lessons to be learned from the national experience. Government clearly can be effective. At times *only* government can be effective. For example—as the UK and Chile have discovered in the last few years—no privatized income protection scheme approaches the value provided by, and the efficiency of, a good social insurance program such as the American Social Security system. Conversely, no health care distribution system based on private insurance, such as exists in the USA, delivers either the quality or the services of the better government systems, which far excel in economic efficiency. In our recent experience, "the pandemics of 1957 and 1968 showed that *voluntary immunization programs controlled and operated entirely through the private health sector were at best grossly inadequate and at worst near disasters.*" Prior to NIIP, "the feeling had been growing that only the federal government could command the resources and impose the guidelines that would be required to mount so massive a venture in preventive medicine."[11]

This understanding has diminished since the advent of the Reagan administration as a highly ideological approach condemning government developed and dominated national affairs, and as both business and government moved to eliminate shared risk and shift it entirely to individuals (except where corporate bailouts are considered essential). Recent ideological excesses, however, seem to be fading, and they did not diminish the truth of the "feeling." In fact, the evidence becomes ever more clear as commitment to privatization becomes ever more disastrous. Examples permeate contemporary experience—Katrina and the virtual loss of a major city, bridges collapsing in the Twin Cities, steam tunnels exploding under streets in New York, food and drug supply of increasingly questionable safety, resources directed elsewhere, and thus unable to deal with the demolition by tornado of Greensburg, Kansas (in this case, fortunately, private resources did jump in later to rebuild the stricken community, and on "green" principles)—and they demonstrate that aversion to government puts American national security at risk.

To be sure, government needs to be controlled to prevent excesses—Kalaupapa springs to mind, as does the seemingly routine killing of young black men by government officials, the police. Nevertheless, government failures in America are overwhelmingly the result of failing to recognize and develop its potential, and of insisting on diluting its effectiveness by relying on the private sector, or even employing public-private partnerships. As the corporate interest in profit replaces the public interest in providing service, the quality of service declines. It is an error to place our health, or our security, in the hands of institutions that exist to generate profit, rather than to provide service. Just as our national security is at risk when we depend heavily upon foreign sources for energy, so our personal security is at risk when dependent upon institutions that profit by denying, rather than providing, service.

As the corporate ethos came to dominate in the health field, the national capacity to handle a severe crisis was damaged. There is no longer the infrastructure to provide care for massive illness throughout the population. There is a shortage of physicians, and a far greater shortage of registered nurses. Hospital beds are lacking. There are no true provisions for emergencies: no adequate shelters, food and water distribution systems, capable response teams, or skilled personnel at all levels with governmental authority.

Americans will never have true national security until they achieve the best, rather than the most minimal, government. Public officials must believe in their tasks; they must be dedicated to making government work, not to minimizing its functions. It is unreasonable to expect officials who believe that "government is the problem" to make government function effectively. Officials who believe that government cannot work cannot be expected to try to make it work. In recent years, our officials have often been more determined to implement ideological agenda than to deliver services or improve their quality. The consequences of this are apparent.

The country is a long way from overcoming years of mismanagement and ideological excess. Ultimately, American security depends upon completely recreating our infrastructure—both physical and institutional, employing delicate monitoring systems, emphasizing broad public education (including health education), and ensuring universal health care.

NOTES

1. Daniel Franklin, "The FEMA Phoenix." *Washington Monthly* (July/August 1995); http://www.washingtonmonthly.com/features/2005/0509.franklin.html; retrieved 22 June 2015.
2. Susan Glassner, and Josh White, "Storm Exposed Disarray at the Top." *Washington Post* (4 September 2005), p. A1.
3. Max J. Skidmore, "Anti-Government is not the Solution to the Probem—Anti-Government Is the Problem: The Role of Ideology in Presidential Response to Natural Disasters from San Francisco to Katrina," *Hazards and Crisis in Public Policy*, 3:4 (December 2012), pp. 12–13.
4. Daniel Franklin, "The FEMA Phoenix," *Washington Monthly* (July/August 1995); http://www.washingtonmonthly.com/features/2005/0509.franklin.html; retrieved 23 June 2015.
5. Phillip Longman, Phillip, *Best Care Anywhere: Why VA Health Care is Better than Yours*. Sausalito, CA: PoliPoint Press, 2007.
6. Franklin, p. 2.
7. *Ibid.*, p. 7.
8. "Exposed by Katrina, FEMA's flaws were years in making," Editorial, *USA Today* (7 September 2005).
9. Eric Holdeman, "Destroying FEMA," *The Washington Post* (30 August 2005), p. A 17.
10. Susan Glassner and Josh White, "Storm Exposed Disarray at the Top," *Washington Post* (4 September 2005), p. A1.
11. Silverstein, p. 22.

BIBLIOGRAPHY

"Alaska: Prince William Sound, Alaska, Earthquake of March 27, 1964," no date. Vibration Data; http://www.vibrationdata.com/earthquakes/alaska.htm; retrieved 17 June 2015.

John M. Barry, *The Great Influenza*. New York: Penguin Books, 2005.

John M. Barry, "1918 Revisited: Lessons and Suggestions for Further Inquiry," *The Threat of Pandemic Influenza: Workshop Summary*. Washington: National Academies Press Institute of Medicine, 2005, pp. 62–63.

Bell, Chief of Staff, Telegram to Commanding General, Department of Columbia, Vancouver Barracks, Washington (19 April 1906), San Francisco Museum. http://www.sfmuseum.org/photos2telegram2.gif; retrieved 15 June 2015.

Olivia Robello Breitha, *Olivia: My Life of Exile in Kalaupapa*, 2nd printing. Honolulu: Arizona Memorial Association, 2003.

Douglas Brinkley, *Gerald R. Ford*. New York: Times Books/Henry Holt & Col, 2007.

Douglas Brinkley, *The Great Deluge: Hurricane Katrina, New Orleans, and the Mississippi Gulf Coast*. New York: Harper Perennial, 2007.

Douglas Brinkley, "Reckless Abandonment," *The Washington Post* (26 August 2007).

David Brown, 2002, "A Shot in the Dark: Swine Flu's Vaccine Lessons," *Washington Post* (27 May 2002), p. A 9.

Chuck Brooks, "The DHS's Role in Confronting Pandemics an Bioterrorism," *Federal Times* (22 December 2014; originally published 4 November); http://www.federaltimes.com/story/government/dhs/blog/2014/12/22/dhs-role-in-confronting-pandemics-and-bioterroreism/20770335/; retrieved 15 July 2015.

© The Author(s) 2016
M.J. Skidmore, *Presidents, Pandemics, and Politics*, The Evolving American Presidency, DOI 10.1057/978-1-137-59959-9

James Lee Burke, *The Tin Roof Blowdown*. New York: Simon and Schuster, 2007.

Carol R. Byerly, *Fever of War: The Influenza Epidemic in the U.S. Army during World War I*. New York: New York University Press, 2005.

Centers for Disease Control and Prevention, "Achievements in Public Health, 1900-1999 Impact of Vaccines Universally Recommended for Children— United States, 1990–1998" (2 April 1999); http://www.cdc.gov/mmwr/preview/mmwrhtml/00056803.htm; retrieved 14 July 2015.

Centers for Disease Control and Prevention, "CDC Advisory," *HAN (Health Alert Network)* 23 January 2015; http://emergency.cdc.gov/han/han00376.asp; retrieved 15 July 2015.

CDC (Centers for Disease Control and Prevention), 2003, "CDC Finds Annual Flu Deaths Higher Than Previously Estimated," Press Release (7 January 2003).

Centers for Disease Control and Prevention, "2014 Ebola Outbreak in West Africa – Outbreak Update," (1 July 2015); http://www.cdc.gov/vhf/ebola/outbreaks/2014-west-africa/index.html; retrieved 4 July 2015.

Centers for Disease Control and Prevention, "2014 Ebola Outbreak in West Africa – Case Counts," (updated July 2, 2015); http://www.cdc.gov/vhf/ebola/outbreaks/2014-west-africa/case-counts.html; retrieved 4 July 2015.

Centers for Disease Control and Prevention, "Measles Cases and Outbreaks," (30 June 2015); http://www.cdc.gov/measles/cases-outbreaks.html; retrieved 15 July 2015.

Centers for Disease Control and Prevention, "Middle East Respiratory Syndrome (MERS)," Page last updated June 5, 2015; http://www.cdc.gov/coronavirus/mers/about/; retrieved 3 July 2015.

Centers for Disease Control and Prevention, "Polio Disease – Questions and Answers," (11 August 2014); http://www.cdc.gov/vaccines/vpd-vac/polio/dis-faqs.htm; retrieved 14 July 2015.

Centers for Disease Control and Prevention, "Polio Elimination in the United States" (29 May 2015); http://www.cdc.gov/polio/us/index.html; retrieved 14 July 2015.

Centers for Disease Control and Prevention, "Severe Acute Respiratory Syndrome (SARS)," http://www.cdc.gov/sars/; retrieved 11 July 2015.

Centers for Disease Control and Prevention, "Vaccines and Immunization" (7 April 2015); http://www.cdc.gov/vaccines/vpd-vac/measles/fs-parents.html; retrieved 14 July 2015.

D. W. Coffman, "U.S.S. Boston," Report to Commander-in-Chief Pacific Squadron, (10 May 1906), San Francisco Museum. http://www.sfmuseum.org/1906/boston.html; retrieved 15 June 2015.

Alfred W. Crosby, *America's Forgotten Pandemic: The Influenza of 1918*. Cambridge, England: Cambridge University Press, 2003.

Alfred W. Crosby, Jr., *Epidemic and Peace, 1918.* Westport, Connecticut: Greenwood Press, 1976.

Kathleen Dalton, *Theodore Roosevelt: A Strenuous Life.* New York: Alfred A. Knopf, 2002.

Mike Davis, *The Monster at Our Door: The Global Threat of Avian Flu.* New York: Henry Holt, 2006.

Christopher Doering, "Egg, Poultry Groups Criticize USDA's Handling of Bird Flu Outbreak," *USA Today* (8 July 2015); http://www.usatoday.com/story/news/nation/2015/07/07/senate-committee-considers-impact-of-bird-flu/29823229/; retrieved 10 July 2015.

Blanche Evans, "1906 San Francisco Earthquake Housing is Valuable Piece of History," *Realty Times* (17 April 20006); http://realtytimes.com/todaysheadlines1/item/8698-20060418_quakehistory; retrieved 15 June 2015.

Laurie Garrett, "The Next Pandemic?" *Foreign Affairs* (July/August 2005), p. 2.

Richard Hofstader, *The Paranoid Style in American Politics.* Cambridge: Harvard University Press 1964; available in numerous subsequent editions.

Carter Evans, "Ebola Panic Spreading Much Faster than Disease in U.S.," *CBS News* (18 October 2014); http://www.cbsnews.com/news/ebola-panic-in-us-spreading-much-faster-than-disease/; retrieved 4 July 2015.

"Exposed by Katrina, FEMA's flaws were years in making," Editorial, *USA Today* (7 September 2005).

Roberto Ferdman, "Egg Rationing in America has Officially Begun," *Washington Post* (5 June 2015); http://www.washingtonpost.com/blogs/wonkblog/wp/2015/06/05/the-largest-grocer-in-the-texas-is-now-rationing-eggs/; retrieved 4 July 2015.

Gerald Ford, "Memorandum for the Heads of Departments and Agencies," 31 March, 1976, "Congressional Relations Office Collection," Swine Flu Folder 1, Box 24, Loen and Leppert Files, Gerald R. Ford Presidential Library.

Gerald Ford, "Memorandum for the Secretary of Health, Education, and Welfare [Mathews]," 6 April 1976. "Domestic Council Collection, James M. Cannon," Swine Flu, April 1–12 1976 folder, Box No. 34, Gerald R. Ford Presidential Library.

Daniel Franklin, "The FEMA Phoenix," *Washington Monthly* (July/August 1995); http://www.washingtonmonthly.com/features/2005/0509.franklin.html; retrieved 23 June 2015.

Brig. Gen. Frederick Funston, "How the Army Worked to Save San Francisco," *Cosmopolitan Magazine* XLI:3 (July 1906), San Francisco Museum. http://www.sfmuseum.org/1906/cosmo.html; retrieved 15 June 2015.

Kathleen Gensheimer, Kathleen, M.D., M.P.H., "Considerations for Pandemic Influenza Planning: A State Perspective," in *The Threat of Pandemic Influenza: Are We Ready? Workshop Summary*, ed. Stacey Knobler, et al. Washington: Institute of Medicine, National Academies Press, 2005, pp. 168–172.

Susan Glassner, and Josh White, "Storm Exposed Disarray at the Top," *Washington Post* (4 September 2005), p. A1.

"Great Work By Signal Corps: Lines are run over Ruined Walls and Through Smoking Streets During Fire," *San Francisco Chronicle* (3 May 1906) San Francisco Museum. http://www.sfmuseum.net/conflag/signalcorps.html; retrieved 15 June 2015.

David Hamberg, "Foreword," in Richard E. Neustadt and Harvey Fineberg, M.D., *The Swine Flu Affair*. Washington: U.S. Government Printing Office, 1978, p. xi.

Robert Himmelfarb, "Letter to President Eisenhower" (19 August 1957), Eisenhower Presidential Library, Records as President, White House Central Files, Official File Box 606 OF 117-T Asian Influenza.

"History of the Medical Department (Excerpted), "Relief Work in San Francisco, California," and "Special Orders No. 37" (20 April 1906), San Francisco Museum. http://www.sfmuseum.org/1906/medical.html; retrieved 15 June 2015.

"History of Quarantine," *The Most Dangerous Woman in America*. Nova website, 2004; http://www.pbs.org/wgbh/nova/typhoid/quarantine.html; retrieved 8 June 2015.

Eric Holdeman, "Destroying FEMA," *The Washington Post* (30 August 2005), p. A17.

Homeland Security Council, *National Strategy for Pandemic Influenza: Implementation Plan*, May 2006.

"Influenza 1918," *This American Life*, PBS, 1998; program description, complete transcript, etc., at http://www.pbs.org/wgbh/americanexperience/films/influenza/; retrieved 7 June 2015; available on DVD from PBS.

Niall Johnson, and Müller Jürgen, 2002, "Updating the Accounts: Global Mortality of the 1918–1920 'Spanish' Influenza Pandemic," *Bulletin of the History of Medicine*, 76:1, (2002), pp. 105–115.

Lyndon B. Johnson, "Transcript of Audio of President Johnson in New Orleans Following Landfall of Hurricane Betsy, September 10, 1965," LBJ Library; http://www.lbjlib.utexas.edu/johnson/AV.hom/Hurricane/audio_transcript.shtm; retrieved 16 July 2015.

Gina Kolata, *Flu: The Story of the Great Influenza Pandemic of 1918 and the Search for the Virus that Caused it*. New York: Touchstone (Simon and Schuster), 2005.

Kevin Kosar, 2005. "Rebuilding Hurricane-Devastated Areas—Why Not Follow LBJ's Lead?" *History News Network* (3 October 2005); http://hnn.us/articles/16383.html; retrieved 17 June 2015.

"Leprosy in Hawaii," undated, typescript from National Park Service; http://www.nps.gov/parkhistory/online_books/kala/pdf/B3LepHawaii.pdf; retrieved 9 June 2015.

Jack London, "The Lepers of Molokai," *Woman's Home Companion* (January 1908); available at http://carl-bell.baylor.edu/JL/TheLepersOfMolokai.html; retrieved 9 June 2015.

Phillip Longman, *Best Care Anywhere: Why VA Health Care is Better than Yours.* Sausalito, CA: PoliPoint Press, 2007.

Anita Manning, "Study: Annual Flu Death Toll Could be Overstated," *USA Today* (11 December 2005); http://usatoday30.usatoday.com/news/health/2005-12-11-flu-deaths_x.htm; retrieved 7 June 2015.

Taylor Maurand, "Feeling Out Leprosy," *Hypercube*, Center for Science and Medical Journalism, Boston University College of Communication (3 November); http://www.bu.edu/phpbin/news-cms/news/?dept=1127&id=41520; retrieved 14 June 2015.

Alice McDermott, "Why Libraries Should Stock *Pale Horse, Pale Rider*." NPR, *All Things Considered*, 23 October 2006.

Victor H. Metcalf, Telegram to President Theodore Roosevelt (26 April 1906), San Francisco Museum, http://www.sfmuseum.org/1906/metcalf.html; retrieved 15 June 2015.

Paul Mickle "1976: Fear of a Great Plague," *The Trentonian* (not dated, but published in the 1990s); http://www.capitalcentury.com/1976.html; retrieved 20 June 2015.

Donald Millar, and June Osborne, "Precursors of the Scientific Decision-Making Process Leading to the 1976 National Immunization Campaign," in *Influenza in America: 1918–1976*, June Osborne, ed. New York: Prodist, 1977, pp. 19–22.

Carla R. Morrisey, "The Influenza Epidemic of 1918," *Navy Medicine* 77:3 (May–June 1986), pp. 11–17; http://www.history.navy.mil/research/library/online-reading-room/title-list-alphabetically/i/influenza/the-influenza-epidemic-of-1918-by-carla-r-morrisey-rn-bsn.html

Adam Nagourney, "California Mandates Vaccines for Schoolchildren," *The New York Times* (30 June 2015). P. A 19.

Richard Neustadt and Harvey Fineberg, M.D., Neustadt, *The Epidemic that Never Was: Policy-Making and the Swine Flu Affair*, (a revised version of *The Swine Flu Affair*, 1978), New York: Vintage Books, 1983; Note: this new edition is not a revised version of the official government report (*The Swine Flu Affair*, Washington: Government Printing Office, 1978). Rather, it is that report, plus additions: it reprints the report, includes a new Foreword by David Hamburg, President of the Carnegie Corporation; a new Introduction by the authors in addition to the original Introduction; and extensive appendices not in the original report.

Richard E. Neustadt and Harvey Fineberg, M.D., *The Swine Flu Affair*. Washington: U.S. Government Printing Office, 1978.

"NINDS Guillain-Barre Syndrome Information Page," National Institute of Neurological Disorders and Stroke (23 January 2008). http://www.ninds.nih.gov/disorders/gbs/gbs.htm?css+print; retrieved 20 June 2015.

NMAH, "Oh Say Can you See: Stories from the National Museum of American History," Smithsonian Institution (16 August 2011); http://americanhistory.si.edu/blog/2011/08/the-history-of-leprosy.html; retrieved 16 July 2015.

Carl Nolte, "The Great Quake: 1906-2006/ Rising from the Ashes," *San Francisco Chronicle* (18 April 2006); http://www.sfgate.com/news/article/The-Great-Quake-1906-2006-Rising-from-the-ashes-2537103.php; retrieved 16 June 2015.

"Pandemics and Pandemic Scares in the 20th Century," National Vaccine Program Office, Department of Health and Human Services (12 February 2004). http://archive.hhs.gov/nvpo/pandemics/flu3.htm; retrieved 7 June 2015.

Katherine Anne Porter, *Pale Horse, Pale Rider.* New York: Harcourt Brace, 1939.

Press Conference: Mathews, Salk, Sabin, Cooper, and Sencer, Transcript, Congressional Relations Office, Loen and Leppert Files, Box No. 24, Swine Flu folder 1, Gerald R. Ford Presidential Library (24 March 1976).

Project for a New American Century (PNAC), http://www.informationclearinghouse.info/article1665.htm; retrieved 22 June 2015.

Howard Pyle to Albert Chandler (25 October 1957), Eisenhower Presidential Library, Records as President, White House Central Files, Official File Box 606 OF 117-T Asian Influenza.

Charles Rabb, "Washington Directs Massive Aid to Alaska Earthquake Victims," *Washington Post* (29 March 1964), p. A6.

David Remnick, "Letter from Louisiana: High Water: How Presidents and Citizens React to Disaster," *The New Yorker* (3 October 2005).

Michael Riccards, *The Ferocious Engine of Democracy: A History of the American Presidency,* 2 volumes. New York: Madison Books, 1995.

Peter Salk, "The Anti-Vaccine Movement is Forgetting the Polio Epidemic," *The Atlantic* (28 October 2014).

Harry Schwartz, "Swine Flu Fiasco," *New York Times* (21 December, 1976), p. 33.

David J. Sencer, and J. Donald Millar, "Reflections on the 1976 Swine Flu Vaccination Program," *Emerging Infectious Diseases,* CDC (5 January 2006), p. 2; http://www.cdc.gov/ncidod/EID/vol12no1/05-1007.htm; retrieved 18 June 2015.

Arthur Silverstein, *Pure Politics an Impure Science.* Baltimore: Johns Hopkins University Press, 1981.

L. Simonsen, et al., "Pandemic Influenza and Mortality: Past Evidence and Projections for the Future," *The Threat of Pandemic Influenza,* Washington: National Academies Press (Institute of Medicine), 2005, p. 105.

60 Minutes, "Swine Flu," (4 November 1979); available at http://www.whale.to/vaccines/swine.html; retrieved 7 June 2015.

Max J. Skidmore, "Anti-Government is Not the Solution to Our Problem, Anti-Government IS the Problem: Presidential Response to Natural Disasters, San Francisco to Katrina," *Journal of Risk, Hazards, and Crisis in Public Policy* 4:1 (March 2013).

Max J. Skidmore, *Maligned Presidents: The Late 19th Century*. New York: Palgrave Macmillan 2014.

Max J. Skidmore, *Moose Crossing: Portland to Portland on the Theodore Roosevelt International Highway*. Lanham, Maryland: Hamilton Books, 2007.

"Special Staff Note" (3 October 1957), Dwight D. Eisenhower Papers as President, DDE Diary Series, Box 27 Toner Notes October.

Howard, Snyder, "Letter to Robert Himmelfarb" (5 September 1957), Eisenhower Presidential Library, Records as President, White House Central Files, Official File Box 606 OF 117-T Asian Influenza.

Michael Specter, "The Deadliest Virus," *The New Yorker* (12 March 2012).

"Specter of 1976," *Effect Measure* (27 October 2005), http://effectmeasure. blogspot.com/2005/10/specter-1976.html; retrieved 22 June 2015.

Kate Stohr, "San Fran's Lessons for New Orleans: How does a broken city pick up the pieces after a catastrophe? Here's what the Crescent City can take from the Great Earthquake of 1906." *Business Week* (12 September 2005).

"Survivors of Katrina Wait for Aid," *Kansas City Star* (14 March 2008), pp. A1 ff.

William Howard Taft, "Telegram to Funston," (18 April 1906), San Francisco Museum, http://www.sfmuseum.org/1906.2apres.html; retrieved 15 June 2015.

Jeffry K. Taubenberger, "Chasing the Elusive 1918 Virus: Preparing for the Future by Examining the Past." *The Threat of Pandemic Influenza: Workshop Summary*. Washington: National Academies Press (Institute of Medicine), (2005), pp. 69–89.

Jeffry K. Taubenberger, and David M. Morens, "History: 1918 Influenza: The Mother of all Pandemics," *Emerging Infectious Diseases (CDC)*, 12:1 (January 2006); p. 1; http://www.ncbi.nlm.nih.gov/pmc/articles/PMC3291398/; retrieved 7 June 2015.

Dylan Tierney, MD and Edward A. Nardell, MD, "Leprosy," *Merck Manual* (February 2014); http://www.merck.com/mmhe/sec17/ch194/ch194a. html; retrieved 8 June 2015.

Kim Tong-Hyung, "WHO: MERS Not Spreading Outside S. Korea Hospitals," *Washington Post* (13 June 1015); http://www.washingtonpost.com/world/ middle_east/who-mers-not-spreading-outside-s-korea-hospitals/2015/06/1 3/9995f426-1230-11e5-a0fe-dccfea4653ee_story.html; retrieved 3 July 2015.

U. S. Census Bureau, "100th Anniversary: San Francisco Earthquake—April 18." CB06-FFSE.02-2, (12 April 2006 reissued); http://www.census.gov/press-release/www/releases/archive; retrieved 23 April 2012.

USGS, "The Great 1906 San Francisco Earthquake," 2006; http://earthquake. usgs.gov/regional/nca/1906/18april/index.php; retrieved 15 June 2015.

Adam Volland, "Lessons From a Bug: A Pandemic Filled Beds but Offered Important Insights," *U.S. News and World Report* (20 August 2007), p. 69.

Acting Secretary of War, Telegram to Commanding General, San Francisco. (26 April 1906). San Francisco Museum. http://www.sfmuseum.org/photos2tele-gram3.gif; retrieved 15 June 2015.

Brian Williams, "LBJ's Political Hurricane," *The New York Times* (op ed) (24 September 2005), p. A

Thomas Wolfe, *Look Homeward Angel.* New York: Simon and Schuster, 1929.

INDEX

© The Author(s) 2016

M.J. Skidmore, *Presidents, Pandemics, and Politics,* The Evolving American Presidency, DOI 10.1057/978-1-137-59959-9

health, education, and welfare, US
  department of, 55
  Office of General Counsel of
    (OGC), 63
Himmelfarb, Robert, 30, 31, 40n15,
  40n16
HIV-AIDS, 3, 26
Hofstadter, Richard, 8
Homeland Security, US Department
  of, 10
Hong Kong, 4, 5
Hong Kong flu, 3, 17
Hurricane Betsy, 43, 46–8
Hurricane Katrina, 25, 36, 38, 44, 46, 48

I
ICF International, 38
immune system, 8, 65
immunization
  inadequacy of voluntary programs
    of, 80
  mass immunization, 61, 65, 70
influenza
  A/Victoria strain in Miami, 70
  dangers from, 34
  death toll from, 3, 16, 17, 74
  pandemics, 15, 17, 71
  seasonal, 60
"Influenza, 1918" (PBS), 21
Iraq, 73

J
Johns Hopkins University Medical
  School, 68
Johnson, Lyndon B., 43, 46–9,
  51n15, 62
  skill in governing, 46
*Journal of Risk, Hazards, and Crisis in
  Public Policy*, 39, 41n35
Justice, US department of, 21, 33, 72

K
Kalaupapa, 26–30, 36, 40n5, 81
Kalawao, 27
Kamehameha V, 26
Kansas, Haskell County, 10, 18, 81
Kennedy, Edward, 69
Kentucky, 31, 32
Kizer, Kenneth W., 79
Kolata, Gina, 23n9, 64, 65, 73, 75n8,
  75n21
Kosar, Kevan, 49, 51n21
Kristol, William, 73

L
leprosy. *See also* Hansen's Disease
  difficulty of contracting, 27
  leprosy colonies, 26
  sulfone drugs, cure for, 29
Leprosy in Hawaii, 28, 40n8
Lewis, David, 53
Liberia, 6
life expectancy, 20
London, Jack, 27, 40n4, 40n6
Longman, Phillip, 79, 82n5
Louisiana, 29–31, 39, 41n34, 48,
  51n17
  Civil Defense Authorities of, 47
Lynn, James, 61

M
Maine Department of Health and
  Human Services, 55
Maine, Ebola panic in, 5–6
*Maligned Presidents: The Late 19th
  Century*, 57n14
March, Peyton, 34–6, 38
"marketplace" attempts at problem-
  solving, 30–2
Mathews, David F., 60–3, 67, 70, 71,
  75n9, 75n12

CPSIA information can be obtained
at www.ICGtesting.com
Printed in the USA
LVOW13*1655311017

554460LV00012B/220/P